Time to Think

Time to Think

Listening to Ignite the Human Mind

Nancy Kline

CASSELL
ILLUSTRATED

First published in the UK 1999 by

Ward Lock

Cassell Illustrated

A Member of Octopus Publishing Group Ltd

2-4 Heron Quays

London E14 4JP

Copyright © Nancy Kline 1999

Reprinted 2001 (twice), 2002, 2003, 2004 (twice), 2006, 2007

British Library Cataloguing-in-Publication Data
A catalogue record for this book is available from the British Library

ISBN 13: 978-0-706377-45-3
ISBN 10: 0-7063-7745-1

Designed by Harry Green
Edited by Ruth Baldwin

Printed and bound in Great Britain by Mackays of Chatham

For Christopher

who is himself a Thinking Environment

Contents

Contents

Part Two
**Creating a Thinking
Environment**

**I. The Thinking
Organization 99**

**II. A Turn of Your Own:
The Thinking Partnership 141**

Acknowledgements

Many people have contributed to the writing of *Time To Think*. I appreciate the hundreds of people whose participation on courses and in thinking sessions over the last decade made possible the discoveries discussed in these pages.

I am particularly grateful to: Jo Adams, Caroline Allen, Tina Breene, Helen Byrne, Frances Fitzgerald, Jane Fitzgerald, Sara Hart, Vanessa Helps, Nancy Hutson, Margaret Legum, Carol Marzetta, Carol Painter, Jerry Polanski, Janice Rous, Christopher Spence and Shirley Wardell for their specific help with the manuscript.

For seeing immediately and saying unequivocally that Time To Think, the new name of my consultancy, should be the title of the book I thank Merl Glasscock. That made the writing possible.

The term Thinking Environment, now a given in this model of human behaviour, was at one time the subject of a frustrating search on my part. Lovell Glasscock resolved that by asking the right question and listening well to the answer. He then said with clarity, 'Why don't you call it a *Thinking Environment*.' I will always be grateful to him for that.

Very special thanks go to my commissioning editor, Deborah Taylor, of Cassell plc, who believed in this book, championed it and created a Thinking Environment for me every step of the way.

Finally, from the fragile, elusive beginnings of this work fifteen years ago right through to the current robust construction of the Thinking Environment process, my husband Christopher Spence has been a central influence and model. His personal communication and his leadership are embodiments of this theory. He is a pioneer, bringing Thinking Environment principles and practice to health care, organizational life, politics, friendship and our marriage. In writing this book I hope to have expressed some of the joy we have experienced in seeing and articulating this process together.

The Thinking Environment

- Everything we do depends for its quality on the thinking we do first.

  Our thinking depends on the quality of our *attention* for each other.

- Thinking at its best is not just a cool act of cerebration. It is also a thing of the heart.

- A Thinking Environment is the set of ten conditions under which human beings can *think for themselves* – with rigour, imagination, courage and grace.

- Listening of this calibre ignites the human mind.

- Between you and a wellspring of good ideas is a limiting assumption. The assumption can be removed with an Incisive Question.

- Incisive Questions increase the functional intelligence of human beings.

- A Thinking Environment is natural, but rare. It has been squeezed out of our lives and organizations by inferior ways of treating each other.

  Organizations, families and relationships can become Thinking Environments again, where good ideas abound, action follows and people flourish.

Time To Think is a comprehensive discussion of this timely, elegant theory and a guide to its model of human behaviour.

Introduction

The day before she died, my mother said a startling thing to me.

'I apologize,' she said, 'for the mess my generation has imposed upon yours. I wish I could have left you a better legacy. I just hope I have left you a measure of courage to face what we have done, and a measure of hope to do something about it.

'But regardless, remember that none of it was your fault. It all began long before you were born.'

My mother was not a sociologist nor a business executive or consultant. She was just an ordinary person, shaken, as I think most people are, by what was happening in the world. I don't know if the mess she was referring to was despotic war, people sleeping in dung on street grates, the sixty-hour white-collar working week, or the end of insect songs as the rain forests burn.

In fact it was probably all of those things. I didn't ask. I just hugged her. I told her that she herself had been for me the greatest legacy of all.

And that was true. She had left me and my sister and twin brother – and every life she touched – with not only the courage to face the mess, but also with perhaps the most important tool with which to do something about it.

Without knowing it, she had also left to the world of business, organizations and government a key to leadership.

She had listened to us.

She had given us time and space to think.

This book is not about my mother. It is not even only about listening – not the way people usually do it. It is, however, about what can happen if you listen as expertly she did, if you ennoble people with the depth of your attention and shake them to their roots by convincing them that they can think for themselves, if you take them into your heart, if you show them that who they are and what they think matter, profoundly.

This book is also about asking Incisive Questions, questions that will remove blocks and allow people to think of things unimaginable before.

With this high-calibre listening and with Incisive Questions people solve problems they thought were hopeless, they build relationships and organizations that host an embarrassment of riches.

My mother's listening was not ordinary. Her attention was so immensely dignifying, her expression so seamlessly encouraging, that you found yourself thinking clearly in her presence, suddenly understanding what before had been confusing, finding a brand-new, surprising idea. You found excitement where there had been tedium. You faced something. You solved a problem. You felt good again.

She was there, present with you, riveted, fascinated by what scintillating phrase might tumble out of your mouth or what idea you might think of that would take her breath away. The process was so supple you did not stop to notice it. You just enjoyed it. In fact, it was not a process to her. It was just the way life was.

She simply gave attention. But the quality of that attention was catalytic. It would be forty years before I would understand the power of what she was doing.

After university, having trained in education, counselling and philosophy, and inspired by Descartes, I set out on a search for the most basic truth I could find. Eventually, I settled on the observation that everything we *do* depends for its quality on the *thinking* we do first. However determined or indefatigable or charismatic a person may be, their every action is only as good as the idea behind it. I could not get away from the fact that *thinking comes first*. It followed then that *to improve action we had first to improve thinking*.

Later I co-founded a Quaker school because my colleagues and I wanted to help teenagers to think for themselves. But we did not really know how to do that. So for several years we observed what was going on when our students thought clearly and for themselves, and what was going on when they did not.

We found that IQ, age, background, gender and even experience seemed to have surprisingly little to do with the times when students thought well. The most important factor in whether or not they could think for themselves, afresh, at a given moment seemed to be *how they were being treated by the people with them*.

We were fascinated to discover that when someone in your presence is trying to think, much of what you are hearing and seeing is *your effect* on them. That was progress, because once we could discover what that thinking-enhancing behaviour was, we could learn it and teach it. Unlike IQ or background, behaviour towards someone was not inherent. It could change.

The faculty puzzled over this. Even the less bright students seemed brighter when they were being treated in certain ways. Over the years, as we teased out the components of this Thinking Environment, my mind occasionally went back to my mother.

I remembered that *the way she gave attention to people had helped them think better, to think for themselves*, sometimes for the first time in their life. I studied my memory of it and began to see the details of the dynamic, its profundity belied so smoothly by the natural way she kept her eyes on my eyes, the way she leaned back and rested her head on her hand, at *ease*, the way she folded her legs up under her skirt and settled in. I noted the tone she used and the sounds she made. I remembered that she had laughed but only with me, never at my expense. I remembered her care for the *place* we lived, how important I felt there.

I re-lived how much her *equal* I had felt and how on most subjects she *encouraged* me to go out to the unexplored edge of my ideas, never seeming alarmed and not seeming ever to compete with me. I remembered, too, how relaxed she was if I should cry or admit to being *afraid* sometimes. I noticed that at certain points, but never intrusively, she would give me *information* I needed. I recalled how much more often she *affirmed* than criticized me, how she *did not interrupt* me or finish my sentences for me, and how her eyes lit up when I found a new and precise way to express something.

I began to see that those simple things had power. My colleagues and I recognized them as a system, one that could be replicated.

The key behaviour was attention.

Much later in my life a chief executive, one of my clients, would sum it up this way: *the quality of a person's attention determines the quality of other people's thinking.*

We reasoned that if the following two statements were true (and they seemed irrefutable),

• everything we do depends on the thinking we do first;

• our thinking depends on the quality of our *attention* for each other, perhaps the most important thing we could do with our life and with our leadership was to listen to people so expertly, to give them attention so respectfully they would begin to think for themselves, clearly and afresh.

Incisive Questions:
When High-quality Listening Isn't Enough

Although the quality of attention people gave each other was crucial, we soon noticed that sometimes listening this well, for all its power, was not quite enough. Something else was needed, something that could take the thinker past blocks that expert attention alone had not been able to dislodge.

Unsystematically, haphazardly almost, we had already been removing the blocks. We knew that the process had something to do with questions. But we did not really know why certain questions worked or how to construct them successfully every time. Nor did we even know what generically the blocks were. We certainly could not yet teach others. We could impress. But we could not empower.

Only after two years of further practice and observation did we see the obvious: that the blocks were almost always *assumptions* being made by the thinker unawares, assumptions that seemed like truth. These limiting assumptions were making it impossible for the thinker's ideas to flow further. Of all the impediments to thinking, of which there are many, these limiting assumptions seemed to be the most deadly.

Soon we saw that there are three types of assumptions and several subsets of those. We determined that being able to recognize the different types of assumptions that are limiting people's thinking helped us to remove them.

We dissected the questions that seemed to work. Eventually we understood them. Their construction had been clean and logical and replicable. Best of all, they were highly teachable.

So over the years we enhanced that basic but mighty listening process with an also-mighty process we call Incisive Questions, so that the human mind, first freed by being paid the highest-quality attention, can also leap past debilitating assumptions, able then to think of things inconceivable before.

The Ten Components

Eventually the essential behaviours which helped people think for themselves became clear. There seemed to be ten, and for the most part they were simple. They were ten ways of being together, ten ways of treating each other. We called this combination the Thinking Environment.

We could see that people do not have to have an IQ of 180, an Oxbridge degree or a sizzling CV to think for themselves with clarity and imagination. They just have to be immersed in these ten things. When they are, they think beautifully. And they act with courage.

The Thinking Environment: A Practical Model

I now spend all my professional life teaching this process. My associates and I, through Time To Think, Inc., teach organizations how to become Thinking Environments. In particular we teach them how to develop team effectiveness this way. We also teach individuals how to be what is called Thinking Partners and to offer each other Thinking Sessions which bring about rapid and dependable personal development. And we teach couples and families how to treat each other this well.

In just about any place where human beings collect and communicate, people find this process works. Some say, in fact, that they didn't think it was possible for human beings to come up with so many good ideas in such a short time. They find also that ideas turn into action more quickly and confidently after they have had time to think in this way. People say they enjoy the inexorable logic of this process, and its beauty.

They say it is just the way life should be.

That doesn't surprise me. I agree that a Thinking Environment is the way life and work and love and everything human was meant to be. I think that our first duty to each other as human beings is to help each other fulfil our nature. And surely the most quintessentially human part of human nature is to think for ourselves. Our minds were designed with the most breathtaking accuracy to do exactly that.

Recently I was enlightened by one woman's summary of a Thinking Environment. She and I were at a business reception together. Earlier that morning, while I was dressing for the reception, I had rehearsed what I would say in case someone should ask, as they inevitably do, 'So, what do *you* do?'

Those moments at receptions are easy to dread because you usually have less than four seconds in which to respond before the eyes of the one asking have meandered elsewhere, scanning the room in that highly refined, networking way for a more prestigious or riveting person to talk to. So as I sprayed my hair, I prepared my four-second answer.

Later at the reception when someone did say, 'So what do you do, Nancy?' I replied, 'I am President of Time To Think, Inc., an international leadership consultancy teaching people in organizations how to help each other think for themselves.' Four seconds.

I smiled. The woman took a sip of wine and said, 'Oh, really? How on earth do you do that?' She was not scanning the room yet.

I was so pleased that I gave her practically my whole opening lecture. And at the end of my pedantic rambling, she said, 'Oh, I see. In other words [she probably meant fewer], if you set up the right conditions, people *will* think for themselves.'

'That's it,' I said, humbled.

Create a particular environment, and people will think for themselves. It is that simple.

We can create a Thinking Environment for each other at any time. We can set up these conditions for each other in our offices, waiting for the bus, chopping vegetables, walking the dog, in the lab, round the fire, on the phone, between the sheets and across even the most mahogany of board-room tables. The quality of our attention and of the Incisive Questions we ask can become just the way life is.

This Book: A Summary

This book is in four parts. Part One discusses in detail the ten components of a Thinking Environment. Part Two describes the two major applications of the theory: the Thinking Organization and the Thinking Partnership. Part Three imagines how five important arenas of human life and work (health, schools, politics, love relationships and families) could change if they became Thinking Environments. Part Four acknowledges our dreams for the world, asserting that *until we are free to think for our-*

selves, our dreams are not free to unfold. The Epilogue pays tribute to Diana, Princess of Wales, suggesting that in public life people have a responsibility to create a Thinking Environment for others.

The Benefits of a Thinking Environment

Turning our world into a Thinking Environment will require the best from all of us. So why should we bother to do it?

Because our days and nights are tightening. Change engorges our organizations; fear constricts our vision. Because in this out-of-control world, it is time for people to think.

Because even though more and more people are saying, 'We don't take time to think about what we are doing; we are too busy doing it', there *is* time to think. In fact, to take time to think is to gain time to live.

We should create a Thinking Environment because it works. Because everything depends on it. And because if you get good at it, you have a tool for life.

I believe that it is time for a Thinking Environment to become the centrepiece of organizations, relationships and families. We have been without it too long. And it shows.

By mastering the theory and skill of a Thinking Environment people do enrich their work, their life and their relationships. Organizations do produce better ideas in less time with better business outcomes. They also increase the motivation and commitment of their work force. And children who grow up in a Thinking Environment do treat others well and live responsibly.

All of this is reason enough to do it. But perhaps most important is the possibility that by taking steps in this way to turn our world into a Thinking Environment, into a place this stimulating, this kind, this alive, this authentic, where no human mind is wasted, and no human heart is trampled, we will not only improve things for ourselves but we may also create a legacy we would be proud to leave.

Part One

A Thinking Environment:
Its Ten Components

CHAPTER 1

Why a Thinking Environment Matters

**Thinking for yourself
is the thing on which
everything else depends.**

No one could stop Dan. It was against the rules. It was his turn to speak and no one was allowed to interrupt him.

I watched the Thinking Environment meeting format save thousands of lives and millions of dollars that day.

It was the Thinking Environment team development day for Dan's team. The company had been developing a drug for over two years. The executives were impatient for the prototype to be finished and put into clinical trials. Most of the people on the team agreed that if they waited much longer to get it out, their rival company would beat them to it.

On this second day of the Thinking Environment course I was coaching the chair of the meeting. People arrived seeming robust. Dan, the toxicologist, however, looked worried. But they said Dan was always worried. They said he was hopelessly negative. A frequent hidden agenda item was to side-step Dan.

One of the components of a Thinking Environment is *equality*. Another is *listening* with respect and without interruption. Another is *removing limiting assumptions*. Another is *appreciation*. This means that everyone at certain points, including at the beginning, has a turn to speak without interruption and with respectful attention from everyone else.

We began. As required in a Thinking Environment the chair opened the meeting by focusing on something positive in the team's work together. Going systematically around the group, she asked everyone to say what they thought was going well in the project. They all did this adequately. But Dan turned to me at the end of his turn and said, 'Do we ever get to say anything negative in this Thinking Environment thing? Do we ever actually deal with problems?'

'Yes,' I said. 'The positive beginning means that people then deal with the problems better.'

Dan nodded, not entirely hiding a sneer.

The chair then outlined the agenda and began with the clinical trials item. True to the Thinking Environment model, she went round the group, giving everyone a chance to speak before any discussion could begin. There were twelve people. The first eight said in one way or another that more delay would kill the project. Then it was Dan's turn. As he opened his mouth, I thought about the opening lines of *King Lear*, when Lear starts off furious and just gets more so.

I watched the group. Some rolled their eyes, some looked down and began to doodle. Several sighed. The chair reminded everyone that they had to keep their eyes on Dan and let their faces communicate respect for *him as a thinker*. They straightened up, reluctantly.

I watched Dan. His anger escalated. People looked scared. He said all the things he had been trying to say for months, pointing out the dangers suggested in the laboratory tests. He finally reached his main point. He said, 'This product causes liver lesions in rabbits. If we go to human trials now, it will be very expensive because we are likely to catalyse cancer in humans and then our product will be dead in the water. And all the money spent over these past two years will go down the toilet. We may have to kill this project to avoid killing people.'

This was just what the team did not want to hear. But they had to keep listening because Dan wasn't through. It was still his turn. 'We are a long way off human trials yet,' he nearly shouted.

Then quite suddenly his rage plateaued. He stopped talking. Nobody moved. He looked out past the group towards the window. Fifteen seconds passed. Then he looked down. He still did not speak. I was comfortable with this because I have seen it so many times. It is the productive quiet of the busy thinker. But some of the group shifted in their seats. Ordinarily someone would have shredded his quiet. This time they couldn't.

At the end of an eternity of about thirty more seconds Dan, unbelievably, sparkled. This cynic turned almost sweet. He 'looked up' from his thoughts and said, 'Actually thinking about it now, I think I could get the kinks out of this thing in just under three months. Just give me three months.'

That was it. He was finished. And he looked around the group. His fresh face seemed to say to the exhausted faces of the others, 'Hi! So what's the matter with you guys?'

The chair, visibly shaken, said, 'OK, well, let's keep going around. Ahmed?'

Ahmed sat up in his chair and took a deep breath, shook his head and then said, 'I can go with three months. I was assuming it would take eight.'

And the next person said, 'Three months, no problem.'

And to a person everyone agreed.

Still rattled, the chair summed up the decision, and glanced down at her Thinking Environment 'cheat sheet'. She said, 'It says here that all of us have a turn now to say what we thought was good about today's meeting and then to say what we respect about the person on our right. So, Doug?'

They did it squirming but with sincerity. As always it worked. And the meeting was over.

I heard Dan say as he walked out of the room, 'Well, what happened? How come nobody blasted my head off today?'

And the chair asked me afterwards, 'Can it have been that simple? Did the meeting work well just because everyone had a turn and we did not interrupt – because we listened?'

Yes.

When I hear about the safety of that compound now, I think about that meeting.

A Thinking Environment is the set of conditions under which people can think for themselves and think well together. They make it possible for people's thinking to move further, go faster, plumb insights, banish blocks and produce brand-new, exactly needed ideas in record time. These conditions are analysed in detail in Chapters 3–12.

We can provide a Thinking environment for each other anywhere, at any time. But first we have to decide to take the leap. We have to be willing to think for ourselves.

CHAPTER 2

Thinking for Yourself

**Thinking for yourself
is still a radical act.**

Thinking for yourself is not a popular activity, though it should be. Every step of real progress in our society has come from it. But in most circles, particularly in places that shape our lives – families, schools and most work places – thinking for yourself is regarded with suspicion. Some institutions thwart it on purpose. It can be seen as dangerous.

I was reminded of this sad fact at a when a fellow guest asked me the subject of a book I was planning to write. I told him that it was about how people can help each other to think for themselves. 'Oh dear,' he said, 'I don't think much of that; I much prefer people do as they're told.' I later found out that he is the fourth-generation president of one of the world's largest oil companies.

When was the last organizational vision statement you saw that included the words '. . . to develop ourselves into a model environment in which everyone at every level can think for themselves'? For that matter, when was the last time somebody asked you, 'What do you really think, *really*?' and then waited for you to answer at length?

This dearth should not surprise us. Hardly anyone has been encouraged, much less trained, to think for themselves, and their teachers and parents and bosses weren't either. And neither were theirs. (We may have learned to revere thinkers like Socrates, but we also learned that the state poisoned him for thinking for himself: not unmitigated encouragement.)

Occasionally, however, we do have a teacher or mentor who truly wants us to develop our own thinking. They give us glimpses. When I was thirteen years old, I was put into an advanced algebra course. On the first day the teacher, who was maligned by students as a hard teacher because she tried to get them to think, stood in front of the blackboard and said, 'On the paper in front of you write the sum of a number.'

The entire class of thirty-five pubescent people just stared at her. She repeated the direction. 'Write the sum of a number.'

I remember my hand gathering sweat around the pencil. A few heads looked down and their pencils started up. I wondered what in the world they were writing. I saw the girl across the aisle from me lean forward and peer over the shoulder of the boy in front of her who was scribbling something. Then she scratched a figure and immediately covered it with her hand.

The teacher paced and rubbed the chalk between her fingers. I wondered what she was about to put on the board. I was now the only one not writing. I leaned back and over my left shoulder whispered to my friend, 'What is it?'

'Seven,' she whispered back.

So I wrote '7' on my paper. I kept my head down, hoping I looked busy and confident.

After the agony among us had become tactile, the teacher asked us for our answers. The number 7 was prevalent. She walked slowly over to the board and wrote: 'There is no such thing as the sum of a number.'

I knew that.

Why didn't you write it?

Sarah said it was 7.

Why did you ask her?

Because – I don't know.

That's right. From now on, think for yourself.

I was too scared around that teacher for the rest of my young life to think very well in her presence. But I took the message with me and gradually examined and valued it. I don't recommend humiliating people into thinking for themselves as she had. She certainly did not create a Thinking Environment for us. Had she affirmed our intelligence first and spoken about the joy of thinking for ourselves, had she not fanned our fear of her, we would all have learned even more powerfully what it meant to do our own thinking. And we might have been able to think well around her too.

But at least she introduced the concept into my academic life. That would not happen again for a long time – not until I was seventeen, when my English teacher required us to write an in-class essay on one of the following two topics:

1 How would you propose we restructure the lunch period?

2 What would change in the world if the men had the babies?

She allowed us thirty minutes in which to do this.

What would change in the world if the men had the babies? I thought she was kidding. She said she wasn't. This was in 1963, and in Dallas, Texas. Nobody I knew for a thousand miles on either side of that city was asking questions like that. The only explanation I could imagine was that my teacher did not like her periods and wished them on men, or perhaps that, contrary to what my mother had said, my teacher *could* remember the pain of labour in childbirth and also wished that on men. I had no idea what she was getting at. So I wrote about lunch.

It was nearly thirty years later before I realized that she had asked an extremely important question. And it was to that memory I went back when I began searching for what to do to encourage people to explore their own thinking and to express it. That teacher set the choice before me – to think about mundane things or big things, but in any case to choose to do my own thinking. There was no humiliation from her ever and no judgement. I decided a year later that I wanted to be an English teacher when I grew up.

Teachers like those two women are rare. It is unfortunate, because even outside education, right inside organizations and work places and families, everyone could be a leader or mentor who sets things up for people to think for themselves. But typically, even when we are in groups that are brainstorming or exploring new ideas, often the unstated warning in the culture is: 'Think the way others are thinking. Think to impress. Think to avoid ridicule. Think to get a promotion. Think to out-manoeuvre.'

We make fun of ideas that are too unusual. We avoid people whose ideas could be seen to be undermining the *status quo* and, by implication, our own status. We also assume that the best help we can be to people is to do their thinking for them, to give them our ideas, to interrupt them and tell them what to think. As professionals we have even been trained to do this, to see ourselves as the experts on what people should do and think. Some people don't actually know what it means to think for themselves. I have worked with individuals and with groups who find the question, 'What do you really think?' profoundly unsettling, even invasive.

Early Roots

This hugely bad habit of not thinking for ourselves and of making sure others don't either still starts young. I saw it graphically in a group of teenagers on a leadership course I was running in London a few years ago. As we began, their faces were open, their energy high. I asked them to take turns answering this question: 'What was a time this year when you demonstrated some kind of leadership?'

Their faces slowly contorted. They looked at me as if I should explain. But what was there to explain?

'What do you mean exactly?' one of them finally asked me.

So I tried to say it differently. 'What did you do this year that required you to take initiative or lead the way?

Still no nod. 'Well, like what sort of thing?' another asked.

'I don't know,' I said. 'That is for you to say. Say what you think. How did you behave like a leader?'

Short silences like this are long. They stretch till they squeak. No one looked down or moved.

'I don't know what I did to lead this year,' said one of the boys finally. 'Hey, Jay,' he said to the boy next to him, 'What would you say I did as a leader this year?'

'Not much,' said Jay grinning. There was a collusive chuckle around the group.

'No,' I said, 'the point is to say what *you* think. You are the only one who knows what *you* think – about this or anything.'

'Yeah, well, that's not as easy as you might think,' said a girl called Bristol. 'Whoever thinks about this kind of thing anyway? I mean, it is not exactly your everyday question, you know. It seems a little bit stupid to me. Who cares how I have been a leader this year? It's like, *I am not exactly on the news every night, am I*?' Some of the others giggled.

'Yeah, I agree,' said another. 'Let's change the subject. This is kind of boring already. Is this what we are going to do all day?'

I knew I had less than ten seconds to re-establish the morsel of credibility I might have had when they arrived. But I could not figure out what had happened. What could have made the question seem boring to them? Unusual, perhaps. But boring?

Then I remembered – boredom can set in because the person is disconnecting from the truth. These young people were doing exactly that. They were running fast from what they actually thought, trying hard to figure out what they were supposed to think, what, in other words, everyone else thought. It was as if their eyes were joined underneath the skull by another pair of eyes like a kind of periscope, scanning the faces of the others in the group to see what the right answer was, the right answer being whatever would not draw ridicule from anyone. The gingerly, almost illiterate dialogue some were venturing with me was actually a sophisticated ritual of fitting-in. It did not seem to occur to even one of them that *thinking for themselves* was a real option.

Probably no post-war mine field could have been more threatening to this group of young people than this terrain between any one of them and the rest of the group. I suspect that when teenagers complain of being bored so much of the time, it is likely to be tied to the all-consuming activity of trying to be someone else. This is probably true for adults too.

So I said, 'When was the last time someone asked you what *you* think?' And slowly, slowly they began to talk. I'll never forget what Lisa said: 'No one ever has asked me that question. I do remember my dad saying not to get smart with him when I had an opinion. He said it was a sign of disrespect. And he had the back of his hand to prove it.'

Lisa and Bristol, like most people, went through their entire childhood and most of their teen years learning how to fit in rather than to think for themselves. They said they did not want to be relegated to nerdhood. They did not want to lose their friends.

As children we learn to look to authorities to do our thinking for us. Then from the minute we make friends we look to them for what to think. Wherever we are, we look around, check out the scene and think what we imagine others are thinking, what we are expected to think. Even at the graduate level, schools teach us ever more sophisticated ways of doing this. Most religions require it for salvation.

In the corporations and governments and families that employ me as a consultant I watch those 'fourteen-year-olds' in the discussions. As middle-aged Bristols they are looking around. They are sussing it out: what are they *supposed* to think here, what will keep them in favour with the people who hired them, who appraise their performance, who determine how fine a school they can choose for their children, who vote for the winners of the professional prizes? Doing what everyone else does, thinking what everyone else thinks is rewarded.

Some people tell me that they are afraid of their own thoughts, that they prefer just to keep on going rather than to stop and think about what they are doing. They fear the upheaval, they say, that may result from finding out what they really do think. The *status quo* is safer.

Thus, at this moment in human history, thinking for yourself is still a radical act. And until we decide that we must do whatever it takes to stop abdicating our thinking, until we see that our *real* survival depends on thinking for ourselves, we will look through those teenage periscopes in every meeting and in every relationship for the rest of our life.

Thinking for yourself is the only reliable road to real safety. Thinking for yourself leads to more happiness, not less. It offers more, not less, respect between you and the people with whom you live and work and whom you love. People may tell you in subtle ways that doing your own thinking is dangerous, but what is really dangerous is to keep on not doing it. To keep tightening our vast minds until they cannot breathe constricts our society and our souls.

If you dare to be radical in this way, to do your own thinking every day, and to help others to do the same, lastingly good things will happen. New ideas that work well, ideas that have been needed for ages, will emerge. Systems that we revere but are hurting us will be exposed and replaced with better ones. Misunderstandings will fade. You will enjoy the fun of it.

But given the misgivings people have about doing this 'thinking thing', this most natural and beautiful and necessary thing, we need the right conditions under which to do it. That is why the piecing together of the Thinking Environment has kept me riveted for years.

The Ten Components of a Thinking Environment

1 **Attention** Listening with respect, interest and fascination.

2 **Incisive Questions** Removing assumptions that limit ideas.

3 **Equality** Treating each other as thinking peers.
   • Giving equal turns and attention.
   • Keeping agreements and boundaries.

4 **Appreciation** Practising a five-to-one ratio of appreciation to criticism.

5 **Ease** Offering freedom from rush or urgency.

6 **Encouragement** Moving beyond competition.

7 **Feelings** Allowing sufficient emotional release to restore thinking.

8 **Information** Providing a full and accurate picture of reality.

9 **Place** Creating a physical environment that says back to people, 'You matter.'

10 **Diversity** Adding quality because of the differences between us.

CHAPTER 3

Attention

Listening of this calibre
ignites the human mind.

The quality of your attention
determines the quality of other
people's thinking.

I have listened to lots of people over the years – most of them professionally and some just because we were together. I don't know of one
person among those many who, under the right conditions, didn't have
interesting and important things to say.

Colleagues sometimes ask me whether I ever get bored listening to
people. Yes: under one circumstance. If people are not saying what they
really think, when they are chronically ducking and censoring or trying
to impress or placate, I am bored. But if people are thinking for themselves about things that really matter to them, I am fascinated. You can
tell when a person has just moved from let-me-please-you thinking back
to their own mind – they go from soporific to scintillating just like that.
I enjoy those moments hugely.

Beneath the fear of being punished for thinking for themselves, most
people have ideas that matter, ideas that would make a difference if they
could be developed fully. People, regardless of their position or status, can
think of things that move discussions to whole new levels of sparkle and
resolution. Individuals you would never suspect of being interesting have
absorbing stories to tell and disturbing insights that would humble even

the most long-winded of us right out of our self-importance and rush. If the conditions are right, the huge intelligence of the human being surfaces. Ideas seem to come from nowhere and sometimes stun us.

The best conditions for thinking, I assumed for years, were hypercritical, competitive and urgent. Schools, organizations, governments and families convince us of that. But in fact it is in schools, organizations, governments and families that people do some of their worst thinking. That is because the conditions for thinking there are usually appalling.

The best conditions for thinking, if you really stop and notice, are not tense. They are gentle. They are quiet. They are unrushed. They are stimulating but not competitive. They are encouraging. They are paradoxically both rigorous and nimble.

Attention, the act of listening with palatable respect and fascination, is the key to a Thinking Environment. Listening of this calibre is enzymatic. When you are listening to someone, much of the quality of what you are hearing is *your effect on them*. Giving good attention to people makes them more intelligent. Poor attention makes them stumble over their words and seem stupid. Your attention, your listening is that important.

We think we listen, but we don't. We finish each other's sentences, we interrupt each other, we moan together, we fill in the pauses with our own stories, we look at our watches, we sigh, frown, tap our finger, read the newspaper, or walk away. We give advice, give advice, give advice. Even professional listeners listen poorly much of the time. They come in too soon with their own ideas. They equate talking with looking professional. Corporate leaders can be the worst. I even knew one chief executive who worked a puzzle when someone came in to see him. It was not uncommon for him to interrupt the person with a loud 'There!' when he found the missing piece. But he had lost the thinking potential of his employee, and their respect.

Listening to each other, if you want to think for yourselves, requires discipline and the most profound attention for each other.

Let's say it is mid-morning. You are busy as usual. The phone rings and the caller says, 'Hi, do you have a minute? I've got a problem. I could use your help.'

You say, 'Sure.' You gear up to be helpful. You get ready to solve the person's problem for them. It would seem logical that if they had any ideas of their own about this problem, they wouldn't have called you.

They arrive. They sit down. You ask them what's up. They begin to speak. And before they have even remotely finished describing the problem, somewhere between their twentieth and fiftieth second of speaking, you figure out what they should do. And you tell them.

They needed ideas. They rang you. You gave them yours. Good? Probably not. Certainly not so fast.

Go back. Notice that, just after you hung up the phone, an assumption raised itself from the land of creaking social indoctrination and told you what to do. It said, 'Helping people always means giving them your ideas.' You assumed that the caller's brain, the one that contained their problem, did not also contain the solution. You assumed, because you had been taught this almost since you could breathe, that helping people means thinking for them. The thing you would do, therefore, would be to listen only as long as it took your brain to think of an idea for them. Then you would say it, expect them to see the genius of it and be grateful.

And over the weeks that followed, you would notice that they were still struggling with the same problem, still trying to solve it. You would privately think of them as stupid or at least stubborn. You would shake your head and walk on. Something had not worked. They had not done what you said. Or perhaps they had and were still not satisfied. This was not necessarily because your ideas were bad; they may well have been perfectly good.

But your ideas were not *their* ideas. And so they were not quite as good – not quite as accurate, as rich, as just right as theirs would have been – because it was their problem, not yours. Also, because your ideas were not theirs, they were less likely to act on them than they would have been if the ideas had been their own.

It was because the teaching, handed down to you with all good will, that the best help we can be to people is to tell them what to think, is not true. It is popular. It is immediate. But it is wrong.

Real help is different. Real help, professionally or personally, consists of listening to people, of paying respectful attention to people so that they can *access their own ideas first*. Usually the brain that contains the problem also contains the solution – often the best one. When you keep that in mind, you become more effective with people. And people around you end up with better ideas.

This is not to say that advice is never a good thing or that your ideas are never needed. Sometimes your suggestions are exactly what the person wants and needs. Many times a robust exchange of ideas is perfect for the task.

But don't rush into it. Give people a chance to find their own ideas first. That chance will take more time than you probably feel comfortable with. Wait it out longer than you want to. You can always resort to telling them what to do later. You, like the rest of us, are probably expert at that.

To help people think for themselves, first listen. And listen. Then – listen. And just when they say they can't think of anything else, you can ask them the question, 'What else do you think about this? What else comes to mind that you want to say?' Even when people are sure there is nothing left in their weary brain, there nearly always is. Surprisingly the simple question, 'What else do you think about this?' can usually lead them straight to more, often good, ideas. In the presence of the question, the mind thinks again.

The next time someone asks for your help with a problem, remember that the brain that contains the problem probably also contains the solution. Then set up the conditions for them to find it.

Andrea was a niche entrepreneur. She grew rare herbs. After twenty years in corporate leadership she had left to follow her heart. She wanted to find a way to combine art and health in one perfect product. These fragile leafy clusters were it.

Three posh restaurants had just commissioned her herbs that week. She was thrilled. I never knew anyone more focused or full of fire than Andrea. Then she came to me one day listless.

'I have a business plan. But I am not doing it. It is sitting there on my table, snoozing. This is not like me. I don't know what to do to get myself in gear on this.'

I had two choices. I could tell her what to do or I could listen. The choice wasn't all that hard. For one thing I didn't know even two measly things about herbs. And telling a dynamo like Andrea just to get on the stick and stop procrastinating was like screaming at Apollo to lift off. So I listened. And was I glad that I had.

Andrea did the most amazing thing with my attention. 'I grow these green babies in my back garden. I like that,' she said. 'That is why I left Alcon, so I could have control over my days and be home in every sense. I have plenty of room and the growing's excellent. Clients are pleased. Now, to expand, I need to have an Open Day, a sort of micro-Chelsea Herb Show this spring in my garden, and this little business of mine will take off. I know it.

'But I keep not organizing the show. It is maddening. My husband Jacob says I am a Meyers Briggs E and need outside stimulus to get me going. No internal discipline. He's wrong about that. I have always been my own best motivator.'

Andrea suddenly went quiet. She look out across the room and leaned forward in her chair. I said nothing. A half-minute passed. I did not move. Something was happening.

'Maybe I am just disorganized. I need someone to come in and be my time and space manager. I could already afford that. I need someone to pick up that business plan and hit me over the head with it and then march me around until I get the herb show started.'

I still did not speak.

Andrea sat back. 'No, that is not it. I am plenty organized. That is not the problem. And I would just maul the person if they came in like that. I would hate it.'

She looked out into the space of my office again. I followed her eyes with mine and imagined what I could not see: the uncountable twinkly things firing off of each other back there somewhere, in that chamber of her mind off limits to me. She was working. Still, quiet, but busy.

Her face smoothed. Her eyes closed. 'I know what the problem is,' she said slowly. She was quiet again. 'I will have to be open if I do that plan. I will have to open my garden. I will have to open my house, my space, my solitude, my heart. I don't know if I can do that. I have put it off most of my life, opening up. It is easy in corporate life and in upper-class Bangladeshi culture and in Britain to stay closed.

'That's it. I will have to be open if I pick up that business plan. Thanks. I can do something about this now.'

Can you imagine what a waste of time and brains it would have been if I had crashed into her thinking process with insignificant advice about 'just doing it'? She would have argued with me, gone home, looked at the business plan and taken a nap. I wanted to say when she thanked me that I hadn't done anything. But by now in this long search to understand a Thinking Environment I knew different.

Interruption

What is it about interruption that is so tantalizing? We seem unable to resist doing it. I once asked a group what they were assuming that made them interrupt their colleagues. They listed these things:

- My idea is better than theirs.
- If I don't interrupt them, I will never get to say my idea.

- I know what they are about to say.
- They don't need to finish their thought since mine is an improvement.
- Nothing about their idea will improve with further development.
- I am more important than they are.
- It is more important for me to be seen to have a good idea than it is for me to be sure they complete their thought.
- Interrupting them will save time.

I almost gasped when I heard a senior manager say while interrupting one of his direct reports in a meeting once, 'Steven, let me just develop the idea you were about to have.'

Finishing people's sentences for them should be studied by epidemiologists. It is a behaviour that has taken over our relationships. We do it to each other all the time. What is the rush? Why is it so difficult just to breathe out and let the person finish their own sentence for themselves?

Tailgating in this way is an insult. When you finish someone's sentence for them you are assuming

1 that they cannot finish it themselves before the world ends;
2 that your words will be their words or better;
3 that it won't hurt them if you do and waiting another giga-second for them to finish will damage you.

Silly, isn't it? None of these bears out.

In fact, most of the time we are wrong about what the person is going to say. Usually they come up with a completely different word or phrase. Often they find in their own mind a much more rich expression. They nearly always come up with a word or phrase that is more precise, more colourful, more *theirs*.

A friend illustrated this point dramatically. She said, 'I am stumped about Larry. As his manager I think I should recommend that we fire . . .' She stopped mid-sentence. I waited a polite three seconds, started to supply the word 'Larry' just as she said, '. . . up his imagination and natural talent a bit more.' I was glad I had not spoken; I would have been not only pedestrian but wrong.

However, what really matters here is not just that the chances are high that you will be wrong when you finish the person's sentence for them. The important thing is *what happens for them* because you let them do it themselves. Even if you are right about the word they are looking for, which you rarely will be, it does not matter. What matters is what happens in their mind, in their own understanding of what they are saying, *because they say it.*

So sit back and let them search. The search and the saying add to the quality of their thinking, to their process of understanding, of sorting things out, of gaining insight. The point is not the word. The point is their internal experience. Only they can do that. Like almost everything in a Thinking Environment, you cannot do it for them. And 'staying out of their way' nearly always takes less time and produces more.

To be interrupted is not good. To get lucky and not be interrupted is better. But to *know* you are not going to be interrupted – that is categorically different. That is bliss. To *know* you are not going to be interrupted allows your mind to dive, to skate to the edge and leap, to look under rocks, twirl, sit, calculate, stir, toss the familiar and watch new ideas billow down. The fact that the person can relax in the knowledge that you are not going to take over, talk, interrupt, manoeuvre or manipulate is one of the key reasons they can think so well around you.

Your Face

One of the surprising players in this level of listening is your face. The difficulty with our faces is that we live behind them. We can't see them when they are in action. And so we don't really know what they are doing half the time. In fact, we often think they are doing one thing when they are off doing something entirely different. That is dangerous because you may think your face is saying, 'Keep going, I am interested', when actually it is saying, 'I am tired of you, go away'; or 'I am threatened by what you are saying, change the subject'.

These expressions are unintentional because you learned them in childhood from your family who wore them unawares too. Those unconscious attitudes were the mode in which your family survived the currents of life. And now, while you are paying attention to someone, you assume you look encouraging, but you may well have slipped into an unconscious 'family' face of worry, fear, disgust, or cynicism.

Your face is a force of encouragement or discouragement. If you look bored, the Thinker will be boring. If you look scared, they will censor. If you seem angry, they will tiptoe. If you worry between your eyes, they will stop and begin to take care of you.

Right now get an expression on your face that you think would encourage someone to keep thinking out loud for themselves, an expression that would say, 'You are good. I am interested. I am not in a rush. Keep going.' Get that expression firmly on your face. Now freeze it. Hold that expression just like that. And put this book down. Walk over to a mirror and look. Would you 'keep talking' to a face like that? If not, change it. And memorize the change.

Your face matters. It can determine where people dare venture. If that seems like a lot of responsibility to put on one ordinary small part of the body, it is. So try not to frown or tighten. But remember that unconscious rigid nicey-nice is just as inhibiting of a person's thinking as unconscious rigid concern or impatience. The point is to be interested and to show it. And not to be artificial. Be yourself, your truly interested, respectful, fascinated self. Learn how to make your face show it.

Your Eyes

'Keep your eyes on the eyes of the person thinking, no matter what. Don't look away even for a second. If there is a fire, I will let you know.

Otherwise, unless you have a seriously unsavoury personal emergency, keep your eyes on their eyes.'

This is the first direction I give people on my courses. It is a basic indicator of attention. Their eyes will go any number of places, but yours must be on them. (If you are blind, you will do the equivalent of this. You will keep your face and head and body profoundly attentive.)

I'll tell you a trade secret here. The Thinker will very likely look away quite a lot. That is natural. Everyone has a personal pace of looking away and looking back. It is a bit like a fingerprint or voice pattern. The pace is uniquely theirs, and it is easy to spot.

Some people look away for a full minute or so and then look back. Some look away for only two or three seconds and then look back. Some people, annoyingly, look away for many seconds and then, without turning their head back to you, move just their eyeballs to look at you again. You have to be on your toes with those people.

Learn the pace of the person you are listening to, because while they are looking away, you can fix your face. You can scrunch it all up, open it wide, pucker, smile, frown, stretch it thin in a second and be back to a relaxed, natural, welcoming look by the time the person looks back at you. (Be sure you have memorized their looking-away pace first, however. You can imagine their shock if you are in the middle of a scrunch when they look back.)

Cross-cultural Thinking Partnerships

Eyes on the eyes of the Thinker got me into trouble once. And I learned vital things from that humiliation. It was in the days before I had properly begun to develop the Thinking Environment model. I was running a peer counselling course in Sydney and had just given what I thought was a show-stopper lecture on listening, having been particularly eloquent, or at least instructive, on the subject of eyes.

When I finished, an Aboriginal woman stood up. She said, as respectfully as anyone has ever spoken to me, 'Nancy, eye contact is a sign of disrespect in our culture.'

That was one of those moments from hell in a course leader's life when all you can think about is the route home. Before I could speak, which would have been a disaster anyway I am sure, she said, 'After lunch let's have a session and I will show you how we give attention without using our eyes.'

'Thank you,' I said, 'I would like that.' I finished the lecture leaving the eye contact part to everyone's discretion. I couldn't imagine what could replace it, but I certainly wasn't going to be yet another American know-it-all and try to guess.

After lunch, Kath and I met. She said, 'Just sit here next to me. We will begin with silence. I will have the first session. When I feel the need to speak, I will. Until then, and throughout, just listen, think about me and what I am saying, but don't look at me. Feel me. Feel my presence.'

I only half-understood. I am shy about anything that sounds too 'spiritual', too 'new agey'. But I realized instantly that, if anything, her instructions were 'old', ancient in fact, and deserving of my utmost respect. So I did what she said as well as I could. She did not speak for a long time. Rapidly I was learning about the value and quality of quiet, about being with someone so fully you hear them at new and profound levels. The session was successful in every way.

As I walked away from that time, I knew I had been in the presence of something almost wholly foreign to my white, western, objectify-them culture. I sensed I had been treated to only a minuscule amount of what was probably an unimaginable depth of human connection, still intact in native societies. Eyes were, in a way, superfluous there; eyes were actually everywhere. Eyes were in our skin and breathing, and in our respect for each other. Eyes were in our interest in what the next thought would be. My thoughts were on her thoughts. Seeing her was an act of being whole. It could not be compartmentalized.

My culture seemed gaunt after that hour I spent with Kath. But I was full. I never forgot it. I long to return.

Nearly a decade later now, I consistently find that Thinking Partnerships can become not only superb places to think, but a way to enlarge our culture by understanding and allowing in the culture of others. So, if you learn my white industrialized cultural way of creating a Thinking Environment and your culture finds any part of it offensive, bring your culture's way of giving total respect to someone, complete and exquisite attention to someone, to change this theory and model.

And if you are from a culture, as I am, in which giving eye contact with a person is a sign of respect, but the person you are listening to is from a different culture, ask them what they do to listen with undivided attention and respect to people. Learn from each other. Your thinking will deepen.

Infantilization

Infantilization is the act of treating someone (including children) like a child, deciding for them what is best, directing them, assuming we know better than they do, worrying about them, taking care of them. In general, infantilizing people means controlling them ourselves, making them dependent on us, requiring them to give over their thinking to us.

You cannot infantilize someone and give them profound levels of respectful attention at the same time.

Infantilization is subtle. Some people explain it as being, in transactional analysis terms, the 'nurturing parent' alternating with 'critical parent'. You infantilize when you want the well-being of another person intensely but you also intensely want to be seen as expert, indispensable and brilliant. Infantilizing others is actually an act of profound insecurity. It looks big and confident, but it is a cover for feeling small and doubting deeply.

Infantilization is the infrastructure of comments like the ones below that I have heard from consultants and other self-described empowerment agents. On their courses these trainers, in the name of teaching, infantilized course participants with comments like these:

'John says he would rather keep his job than say what he thinks. Now how powerful would you say he is being in that situation?'

'When are you going to start facing the truth, Sam?'

'I know you can really, really, really do this, Janice. Your only problem is your self-image.'

'I am here twenty-four hours a day, thinking about you and believing in you. Ring me any time.'

'I know I am right about this. You'd be better off just to trust me on this one.'

'Hi, cutie. How's the up-and-coming star of this organization?'

'You are not leader material but you are a whopping good support.'

In each of those disempowering comments, the trainer is in effect standing over the person, stroking their hair and saying, 'There, there, I know best. I will take care of you, you young thing.'

Patronizing, infantilizing behaviour is difficult to interrupt because it is done in the name of being supportive and on your side, and because it is subtle and unconscious on the trainer's part. Usually they have denied it and claim not to be feeling superior or competitive. 'I just want the best for you, that's all.'

Infantilizing your clients, your friends, your family or your work force prevents their thinking for themselves. This is because attention requires respect. Real respect precludes infantilization. Every component of a Thinking Environment is chosen, therefore, to prevent infantilization. You will see in Part Three of this book that every one of the six parts of the formal Thinking Session is also an act of preventing infantilization.

To infantilize is to belittle the mind.

Co-dependence

Co-dependence and infantilization are cousins. I bring up this concept because co-dependence is a terrible state in which to try to do your own thinking.

There are fifty gazillion books and tapes out now about co-dependence, but just in case you have not come across the term, co-dependence is an addiction to pleasing people. The term was coined in the field of the Twelve-step Programme for addiction recovery to describe the person in an addict's life who is so scared to lose the addict's love that they don't dare challenge the person's addiction. For example, the person who is addicted to an alcoholic will say, when the alcoholic is out cold on the floor every night, 'Oh, that's Jamey for you, always exhausted after a hard day's work.' And for fear of making Jamey angry or risking losing the relationship, the co-dependent will not require Jamey to change the behaviour. In that sense the co-dependent is inside the addiction with Jamey, thus co-dependent.

But co-dependents are everywhere, not just in the lives of active addicts. You are co-dependent if:

- You feel that you are dying (literally) if the person is mad with you.
- You feel joy only when the other person is happy and are sad the minute they feel sad.
- You ask them what *they* think in order to know what *you* think.
- You lie to keep them pleased with you.
- You do not know you exist apart from them.
- You exist in a pool of anxiety when you haven't heard from them.
- You are most happy obeying, most uncomfortable thinking *for yourself.*

This total identification with other people is established early in life. It can attach to any situation; the addict's life is only one. Co-dependence is rampant in any structure requiring obedience or conformity. And that is a lot of places: families, schools, hospitals, government, corporate life and the military, to name a few.

Some addictions are sanctioned. Addiction to work is one. People are required to be work addicts in some organizations. And if not required, they are certainly paid well for it. Some people at the top of organizations are not addicted to work but feel they have to appear to be.

Addiction to authority sets people up to be both addict and co-dependent, not an unusual combination. Likewise with the cultures of marginalized groups. People seek to escape the pain of oppression through numbing addictions or through co-dependent obedience in the hope of acceptance by the dominant group. I see this every day in women's culture – women are rewarded for melding with their mates, for looking to others (usually men) to think for them.

Thus the co-dependent person, coming from whatever background or experience, can make a good listener, because they are most comfortable giving, but they do not at first make a good thinker. To improve markedly, however, they just need to practise thinking for themselves and to test the results in their *real* lives, to *notice* that they were not less loved or less alive when they dared to have their own thoughts, to voice and to act on them. This takes a while, but is exhilarating to watch when it happens.

It is my hunch that the inexplicable resistance some people have to the Thinking Environment process comes from entrenched co-dependence inside themselves, the terror that they will lose everything, even their life, if they detach from the mind of the people they love and begin thinking for themselves. If you identify with even some of the seven characteristics listed above, comfort yourself with the thought that to begin to think for yourself and to offer that great favour to someone else will in the end secure you more acceptance, more real love, more friendships and greater peace than you may ever have known.

If you are co-dependent, you want people to want you. But remember: it is hard for a person to come towards you if you are already smack against their face. Stepping back from people and defining your separate self make it possible for them to move towards you. People, thoughts and water molecules all need space in order to be attracted. Your *own* mind is easy to love once you put it centre stage.

Quiet

The fact that people have stopped speaking does not mean that they have stopped thinking.

If you are lucky, when you are listening to someone, they will suddenly go quiet. It will not be a dead quiet, not flat, or crumbly or desperate. It will almost chime.

When people are quiet in this way, they are busy. They are off on a solitary 'walk'. You have not been invited to come along, but it is assumed that you will be there when they come back. They will want to tell you about where they have been. Their 'walk' is of high quality exactly because they know you are waiting, thinking about them, while they are 'gone'. This is a privileged moment for you: don't ruin it.

You may well feel awkward when the quiet first sets in. You may have been taught that at times like these you must speak, that you must 'rescue' the person from the apparent mounting embarrassment of having nothing to say. Yet when a person is thinking out loud and suddenly is quiet but is not stuck, the quiet is alive. Neither the person nor the quiet needs rescuing. They need attention only – and more quiet.

Listening to their quiet, you will not know *what* they are thinking. But you will know *that* they are thinking. It would take you 32,000,000 years, so say scientists, to count the number of electrical connections that are happening in their wondrous brain during that quiet. And in those connections ideas are forming, insights are melding, most of which you will never hear about.

Soon there will be words again, though. After the quiet, lights shine, both in the Thinker's eyes and in their eloquence. These quiet busy times are when the least *seems* to be happening but the most *is* happening. I think they are now my favourite moments in listening to people think.

As a young woman I watched Quakers in their quiet. Without realizing it I learned about the power of silence, of being present with other human minds as profound things happen. The Quakers would not describe it exactly that way. They would say that each person was sitting in quiet, opening their spirit to the presence of God. Quakers believe that if they sit quietly, God will eventually speak through them.

Aged twenty-two I was way too sure of myself and closed-minded to know how to open myself to the divine, but I did learn important non-divine things from the Quakers during those years. I learned that when people listen to each other with the discipline of Quaker silence and attention, something valuable happens. The practical thing the Quakers were doing was giving everyone permission to speak and then not inter-rupting each other. As a good Quaker you are required to let the speaker finish and sit down before you stand and speak. Even if God is banging at your rib cage with a tonne of urgent messages, you have to wait. The message just given is supposed to settle into everyone's hearts and minds with a sort of printer's white space before the next person may stand and be heard.

It is Quaker culture in those meetings not to interrupt – and not to dominate. It is just the way life is there. And it works. Quakers have been in the forefront of human liberation and advancement for 300 years.

I learned from them. I grew because of them. But I was certainly not trained to be like them. As a young student of the social graces I was specifically instructed over many years to prevent quiet gaps at all costs. I am probably one of the best fill-in-the-blank experts Texas society ever produced. Give me a quiet moment in a person's chat and I can scoop it right up, kiss it to death, fill it up until it is completely transformed into a conversation prize-winner in and of itself.

I was taught that if it is done well, the person who went quiet like that so precariously will probably not thank you, but will, nevertheless, be unconsciously grateful to you for the rest of their life. That put it square in the middle of the 'stars-in-your-crown' category of invisible social service for me: almost a religious duty.

That kind of learning is hell to undo. And it took me years and years. I got good eventually at recognizing the difference between the busy quiet and the dead quiet.

And then I finally got good at allowing the busy quiet to go on 'unrescued' by me. But what took the longest was my truly *enjoying* that quiet. It has been only in the past few years, in fact, that I have looked forward to and revelled in those privileged quiet times.

Consider how long you think you could bear to be quiet and let someone think out loud. With only the occasional benign murmuring and nod and smile of understanding from you and the occasional question requesting even more thoughts, a person in your presence might just turn into a genius – at least, for that moment.

And they will think you are brilliant. They will thank you. You will feel you did nothing, but you will have given life. Like the sun, you will just have come out and beamed. That was all. And look what happened.

CHAPTER 4

Incisive Questions

Incisive Questions remove limiting assumptions,
freeing the mind to think afresh.

There are indisputable beauties in this world. The human mind is certainly one. An Incisive Question to free it is another.

An Incisive Question, crafted with precision and lustre, is any question that removes limiting assumptions from your thinking so that you can think again. An Incisive Question does this by replacing the limiting assumption with a freeing one.

The Limiting Assumption

Let's say you want to talk to Neil, your boss, but you tell me you can't do it. So I ask you, 'What might you be assuming that is stopping you from talking to Neil?' You tell me that you are assuming he will laugh at you and that he will think you are stupid. After more thinking, you realize also that you are assuming that, actually, you *are* stupid.

Those assumptions sit there, a blob in your brain. You go through your whole day, perhaps even your whole week (perhaps your life) not talking to Neil. The assumptions hold you back from doing what you want and need to do. The assumptions limit your thinking and thus your life. The assumptions are simple, but lethal.

Ordinarily, if you were to tell a colleague about this, they would say something like, 'So what if he laughs and thinks you are stupid. You *aren't* stupid. Go on and talk to him!' Feeling battered by the reproach, you nevertheless say OK. But in the end you do not do it; you still put off talking to Neil. Your colleague might be right, but the assumption squeezes you. Telling you *just to do it* won't work.

The Incisive Question

A question, however, will. A question will get rid of the assumption and replace it with one that frees you to think about what to say to Neil and then to say it. A question works because, unlike a statement which requires you to obey, a question requires you to think. The mind seems to prefer to think, not to obey. In true emergencies like fires, ship wrecks and haemorrhages, the human mind obeys happily enough. But in ordinary life the mind wants to think for itself. It resists commands. It responds to questions.

However, just any old question won't do. It has to be a question that *accurately* identifies the assumption and then replaces it with the exactly right freeing one. The key is listening with precision.

If I were your colleague, I would be thinking the following things:

- Your assumption is that you are stupid.
- That is an untrue assumption.
- I will remove that assumption by replacing it with a freeing one: you are intelligent.
- I will put that freeing assumption inside a question and link it to your goal of talking to Neil. The question would then look like this: *If you knew that you are intelligent* (freeing assumption), *how would you talk to Neil* (goal of the session)?

Three Kinds of Assumptions

There are several different kinds of assumptions:

- facts;
- possible-facts;
- bedrock assumptions about the self and about how life works.

55

In Part Three I will go into detail about these different kinds of assumptions and show you how they are removed differently. For right now, however, know that when you spot an assumption that is limiting someone's thinking, you can remove it deftly with a question.

Over the years I have collected Incisive Questions that made a difference in people's lives and organizations. Below are some samples. Note that the first part of the question asserts a positive assumption; the second part directs the Thinker's attention back to their issue or goal.

- If you were to become the chief executive, what problem would you solve first, and how would you do it?
- If you knew that you are vital to this organization's success, how would you approach your work?
- If things could be exactly right for you in this situation, how would they have to change?
- If you were not to hold back in your life, what would you be doing?
- If you found out that someone you love very much is going to die tomorrow, what would you want to be sure to say to them today?
- If you could trust that your children would be fine, what would you do with the rest of your life?
- If you knew that you are beautiful just as you are, what would change for you?
- If you knew that you are as intelligent as your bosses, how would you present yourself to them?
- If a doctor told you that your life depends on your changing the way you live, what would you do first for yourself?
- If you trusted that your excellence will not put others in your shadow, what would your goals be?

You can identify your own assumptions and create your own Incisive Questions to remove them in a second.

If you want to take action, but you are stuck, ask yourself, 'What am I assuming here that is stopping me?' Listen to the answer, which might be: 'I am assuming that I don't deserve success here.' Then remove it: 'If I knew that I do deserve success here, what would I do right now?'

If you want to feel better, ask yourself, for example, 'What am I assuming that is making me feel depressed?' Note the answer: 'I am assuming that I have no choice here, that I am powerless. Then remove it: 'If I knew that I *do* have a choice here and am powerful in this situation, how would I feel?'

Group Assumptions

If your team has run out of good ideas, ask yourselves, 'What might we be assuming here that is limiting our thinking on this issue?' And remember the answer, which could be: 'We are assuming that only the top people can think about this well enough.' Then remove it: 'If we knew that we can think about this as well as anybody, perhaps even better, what would our ideas be now?' In other words, notice the problem, find the limiting assumption and replace it with a freeing one.

Incisive Questions get your mind fired up again. They are simple. Don't make them complicated. They work because they cut to the core.

CHAPTER 5

Equality

> Even in a hierarchy
> people can be equals as thinkers.
>
> Knowing you will have your turn
> improves the quality of your listening.

There is something about reciprocity that creates better conditions for thinking. Reciprocity banishes the assumption that only some people are thinkers. Many people assume that they are not among those clever elite. They assume without even realizing it that their mind doesn't warrant people's attention.

That assumption is not true. In a Thinking Environment, even in a hierarchy, everyone is valued equally as a thinker. Everyone gets a turn to think out loud and a turn to listen. There is no room either for self-sacrifice or for greed. To know you will get your turn to speak makes listening easier. It also makes your speaking more succinct. And to know you will have to listen makes you more open-minded and generous. Equality keeps the loud people from silencing the quiet ones. But it also requires the quiet ones to contribute. In a Thinking Environment no one can abdicate responsibility for thinking.

In organizations people are often made to feel that they should not speak unless their idea is fully formed and acceptable before they open their mouth. They do not dream of taking people's time and attention for the purpose of thinking something through as they speak. Their assumption is that people can't talk about something until they have thought about it first. I believe it is more true to say that people can't think about something until they can talk about it first. The human mind works best when it can hear itself, notice its inconsistencies, be reminded of its quality and take its time. Remembering Charles Handy's book *The Empty Raincoat*, I am reminded of this question: 'How can I know what I think until I hear myself speak?'

Meetings and Teams

Organizations also intimidate people into believing that 'the higher up you are in a hierarchy, the better you can think'. And welding this assumption to the floor of the mind of managers is the assumption that to seek out ideas from people junior to you is to look incompetent. The absurdity of this is obvious – often the people near the top, because of their isolation from what is really happening, have less chance of thinking well than most of the people junior to them – but the assumption persists nevertheless.

Not, however, at Staples, the office supply company. One of the divisional managers has done a good thing. She has institutionalized equality of thinking in the work place. She has set up a forum for ideas, a bimonthly meeting with all levels of her staff. She gathers them in groups of about twelve (which, by the way, is about as big as you can make a group and still expect it to be safe enough for people to say what they think. Organizations that gather two hundred employees to announce policy changes and then open the floor to questions and comments from the audience are, in effect, not holding an open consultative forum at all. Most people will not stand up to speak in a group of colleagues that large).

The Staples manager poses two questions: 'What have you noticed that needs attention or change in this company that I might not have noticed?' and 'What do you think should be done about it?' Then she sits down and *listens*.

Everyone speaks without rush or interruption. She makes notes, asks clarifying questions only, does not challenge their ideas or defend herself. She promises to think about each one. She does not promise to do everything people suggest, but she does agree to let them know what she decides to do with their ideas and why. This takes time, but she claims it has gained time overall because embers have been snuffed before they combusted, new paths she had never thought of have opened up, and employee involvement and commitment have increased – those two unmeasurable soft qualities on which so much of the hard stuff depends.

Equality is particularly a feature in any Thinking Environment meeting. Many times during the meeting, including at the beginning and at the end, everyone has a turn to speak. Every person is considered equally valuable. The chair or other people in authority may have to make the final decisions; not every meeting can work effectively on consensus. But the chance to contribute ideas and points of view is given equally in a Thinking Environment.

This seems basic and obvious to me. If you value only certain people's ideas, don't invite the others to the meeting. And if you don't want anyone's ideas, issue a memo and save everyone a lot of time and degradation. But if you want ideas better than your own and a meeting with better and better concrete outcomes and a team that works splendidly together, invite them all and give everyone an uninterrupted turn to speak and the skills to listen. Every Team Start-up Kit should have this right on the top.

An attitude of equality towards each other expressed in the structure of reciprocity is another strike against infantilization in organizations. You will recall that infantilization (page 47) slows down people's thinking, makes them functionally less intelligent. Seeing people as thinking equals, on the other hand, makes them functionally more clever. The things you learn and the more competent you become by hearing their thinking makes listening to people as equals almost a selfish act. There is so much in it for you.

This is true in families too. I want to preview Chapter 39 by stating here that families are certainly teams. They are actually small (and enormously complex) organizations and can be run beautifully as a Thinking Environment. If parents would treat their children as thinking equals and ask for ideas from them, they would hear astute things often and make better decisions. In fact, if you are a parent, do what the Staples manager did. Ask your children what they think. Listen long and well to them without stopping or arguing with them. Tell them you can't promise to do what they say, but do promise them you will let them know what you do with their ideas and why. Remember, you can always say, 'I appreciate your telling me and I'll get back to you [or something less stilted and businessy than that]. You do not have to rush in with an agreement or a setting-them-straight rebuttal. Listening does not commit you to anything. It can, however, liberate good thinking from everyone and help the family live more happily together.

Respect is the hallmark of a Thinking Environment. Equality is its base.

CHAPTER 6

Appreciation

A five-to-one ratio of appreciation to criticism
helps people think for themselves.

Change takes place best in a large context
of genuine praise.

Appreciation keeps people thinking. Appreciation, when it is genuine, is important not because it feels good or is nice, but because it helps people to think for themselves on the cutting edge of an issue. Repeated criticism does not. In fact, the more controversial or disturbing the subject they have chosen to think about, the more important it is to be sure the thinker knows *specifically* how they are appreciated.

Reality and the Norms

The human mind seems to work best in the presence of reality. The more nearly whole the picture, the better. And reality contains what is good as well as what is bad. In fact in most cases there is, in a complete picture of reality, far more good than bad.

Carol Painter, a management consultant and trainer in Sheffield, developed the Negative Reality Norm Theory. She points out that an accurate picture of reality, according to our society, is considered to be a negative one. Society teaches us that to be positive is to be naive and vulnerable, whereas to be critical is to be informed, buttressed and sophisticated.

Organizations operate on this negative norm. When we introduce the positive, therefore, we are seen to be challenging the norm, to be inserting something extra, intrusive, imported. Whereas, actually, injecting the positive into our picture of reality is an act of *completing* reality, not implanting something foreign into it.

A Thinking Environment completes reality. It requires a balanced picture including the positive truths about a person, group or situation. The mind needs this whole and accurate picture of reality in order to work well.

Giving

One of the ten components of a Thinking Environment, therefore, is called the 'Five-to-one Ratio of Appreciation to Criticism'. When you are paying attention to someone as they think, be sure to indicate with your face and eyes and sounds that you respect them, that you appreciate them as thinkers and as people, even if you disagree with their ideas, and even if you do not particularly like them. You can still respect someone as a thinker, as a person, and not be able even to bear the thought of lunch with them.

Appreciation of someone needs to be *genuine, succinct and concrete.* If you fake it, they will know. If you go on and on and on, they will go numb. If you are too general, they will not believe you.

If you want people to think well around you, succinctly and sincerely appreciate people throughout your day. Notice something good and say it. People need this and benefit from it instantly. One woman told me that it would make the most enormous difference to her if her supervisor would just write an e-mail once a month telling her something she had noticed that she admired in her work – just one sentence once a month. But I have heard professional people say that people with even a modicum of self-esteem do not need to be told positive things. I heard one man say, seriously, 'I told you once (five years ago) and that should be enough. Why can't you remember that?'

Showing appreciation, short, accurate, genuine, is vital. I think we should become seed-sowers of confidence and intelligence in the people around us by doing this simple thing.

Receiving

Occasionally the social graces turn out to be brilliant.

In exploring why it is that so few people appreciate each other directly, I discovered that the problem lies partly with the people being appreciated. They do such a lousy job of receiving. Many people are taught that to be appreciated is the slippery slope of gross immodesty and out-of-control egomania. It's as if when you hear something nice about yourself and don't reject it instantly, you will, *presto*, turn into Donald Trump or something. This is ridiculous.

Being appreciated increases your intelligence. It helps you to think better. So don't do what so many people do. Don't utter a shuffly, hissing 'humph' that is intended to be modesty, but is actually saying, 'I've been told I'll get ego inflation if I don't dismiss compliments like that, and anyway, someone else any second is going to insult me so I might as well insult myself before they get a chance.' Those dismissive responses actually insult the person who paid you the compliment. And insults are a thinking inhibitor.

Just say thank you. Think of it as a gift. It is decent manners to say thank you when you receive gifts.

But don't do it for that reason. Do it because, if you don't, you destroy the Thinking Environment for you both. The chances increase that the person will not compliment you again. The giver generally is being sincere and has thought about what they are saying. To say, 'You are stupid', which rejection does say, is to lower the chances that they will keep thinking well about you.

Also, as the receiver, if you throw the appreciation back in their face by saying 'humph', or 'Flattery will get you nowhere' (do people still say that?) or some other mindless rejoinder, you destroy for yourself the requirement that *you think about* what has just been said and assess it intelligently and perhaps even let it have a positive effect on your thinking. 'Thank you' sustains a Thinking Environment for you both.

Do It Now

Think about someone you appreciate or admire, someone whom you may not have appreciated out loud in a long time, or perhaps ever. Decide what you would like to tell them. Keep it brief and real. Then tell them today. And note their response. If it is dismissive, tell them just to say 'thank you'. If it is warm and receptive, enjoy it. Then do it again in a week or so.

Don't be phoney with this. Being disingenuous is particularly bad in this circumstance. People need and deserve honest appreciation every day, several times. If what they get instead is pretence, they will come to distrust even genuine appreciation. Beware also of watering down appreciation with caveats like, 'I thought you were stupid and ugly at first, but now . . .' Just say the positive thing. Don't put yourself down in the process. Don't say, 'I would give anything to be even 10 per cent as good as you are.' That will make them feel bad for you. Just do it – straight.

And do it before they die. No one's life is guaranteed for a single second. What will you wish you had said to a colleague or friend or lover or child or boss or parent if they should die tonight? No matter how mud-filled your confidence is in this area, shuffle across the floor right now and write them a note or e-mail them or ring them. Tell them. Even if they say, 'What's got into you?,' they will be glad you rang. And so will you in the morning.

Remember, too, that the higher up people are in an organization or family, the more appreciation they need and the less they get. Leadership, with its inevitable panoply of attack, sucks tender self-appreciation right out of people. Find ways to appreciate them. Don't confuse that with flattery. Appreciation is real.

Correcting Behaviour

When you have to give criticism or negative feedback, and we all do, begin and end with something genuinely positive. And focus if possible not on everything that is bad about the thing or person you are critiquing but on the key thing which, if it were to change, would change the rest for the better. In a large context of genuine praise, the person will more readily make the change. Too much criticism drains the mind and the body of the desire to move forward.

Keeping the ratio of appreciation to criticism approximately five to one will keep the person thinking well. I made a rough stab at determining that ratio many years ago in an attempt to move people away from the destructive habits of excessive criticism. My guess at that time was a ten-to-one ratio of appreciation to criticism. People questioned that proposal, suggesting that even a ratio of one to one was challenge enough.

But I felt vindicated last year when I read about the research out of a laboratory in Seattle where it was observed that relationships that last and are healthy are ones in which the ratio of positive to negative interaction is five to one. Even the frequent fighters in relationships that were happy and long were five times more peaceful and supportive with each other than they were bellicose. So I have changed the ratio from ten to one to five to one in my teaching. Five times more positive interaction than negative is still a monumental challenge.

Every day the world pulls us down, shakes us up, slices into us, laughs at our attempts and belittles our triumphs. We legitimately need to hear afresh every day a few things that are honestly good about us. Most important of all, these good things will help us keep thinking for ourselves with courage and clarity. Surely that is a good enough reason to discard the negative norm culture that keeps you from saying what is good and turn to the person next to you with a reminder of their strengths.

Notice what is good and say it.

As with any force for lasting change, it is simple.

CHAPTER 7

Ease

Ease creates. Urgency destroys.

When it comes to
helping people think for themselves,
sometimes doing means not doing.

In the early years of this work I did not include ease in the list of Thinking Environment components. Although some sessions were going better than others, I could not figure out why. Ease is like that, of course. It is a presence defined by an absence. And it was exactly this absence of tension or rush that gave a higher sheen to some sessions. Ease allows the human mind to broaden and reach.

Ease is the space a Thinking Environment needs in order to stay intact.

Yet ease is being systematically bred out of our lives. Ease is seen to be the enemy of the fast profit, the keep-ahead drive, the you-are-what-you-have-and-whom-you-control society. Like a kind of commercial eugenics, the world selects the frenzied, tense leaders to breed, to populate our organizations and to set far-reaching policy for our world. Other models of leadership are 'sterilized out'.

I realized this as if shot awake during one lunch-time consulting job I was doing. Without question one of the most unsettling things I ever heard inside an organization (a revered and idolized multi-national) was this coolly delivered statement from the chief executive: 'I cultivate an atmosphere of urgency around here in order to get the greatest productivity from my employees.' *Cultivate urgency.*

For years I had been assuming that the organizational sickness of rushing everybody to death with impossible production targets, sixteen-hour working days and brief cases disgorging weekend work were an accident. I had thought, stupid me, it was a condition for which every company president would apologize and fix as soon as possible. Not so; it was policy. Well-educated people in power actually thought it was a good idea.

My first employer, a Quaker headmaster, had spoiled me. Thornton Brown knew lots about ease. I remember walking into his office one afternoon during my first year of teaching. He had asked to see me because he had had a complaint from the parents of one of my English students. He was sitting at his headmaster's desk when I walked in.

When he saw me come in the door, he stood and smiled, said hello, set down the copy of *Sailing* magazine he had clearly been reading and then sat again. He leaned back in his chair and said, 'Mrs Andrews called me. She thinks you are corrupting her daughter by teaching D. H. Lawrence in your senior literature class. What do you think?' He always wanted to know what I thought before he offered his view.

I made my university-graduate defence of great literature and said something about Shakespeare being more lewd than Lawrence. Thorny listened and paid attention to me. That man knew in his bones how to create a Thinking Environment for people. I went on a bit more. When I couldn't think of anything else to say, I looked at him with a large amount of twenty-two-year-old first-job fear.

And he stunned me. He said gently and slowly, the way he spoke about everything, 'I don't care which books you teach as long as you remember one thing. The students are learning *you*. They will forget about D. H. Lawrence. But you and your life they will remember. Be sure you like what they are learning. Go back to work. I'll handle Mrs Andrews.'

He smiled. He never raised his voice or lifted his white eyebrows or fidgeted with a thing. He just sat there, showing me what he meant. He was teaching me *him* too. I was learning about ease and about integrity and about seeing what is simply true. I am still learning that from him thirty years later, long after his death. You don't have to be alive to keep teaching if you have taught your life while you lived.

So that chief executive with the urgency clause in his management style shocked me. Because he himself was urgent and because he taught urgency on purpose to his people.

I was heartened a bit, however, when it was the company's employees' turn to talk to me. One by one they said things such as, 'The pace is nuts. And no, it doesn't make us more productive. It shortens our fuse. It makes us dog meat at the end of the day. When we are productive, it is not because of this wedge-it-in, pile-it-on pep policy. It is in spite of it.' One man told me that no one even has *time to think* about what they are doing – they are too busy doing it.

Urgency keeps people from thinking clearly.

Somewhere inside you you know about this. Ease sidesteps knots, disperses crises and like a lever lifts the cargo with the tip of its finger. People who are immersed in ease can see a solution almost instantaneously, because their minds are not gyrating in the middle of tangential, usually imagined, emergencies. And people who are at ease while someone is trying to think in their presence work near-miracles. Ease conceives and grows cymbal-crashingly exciting thoughts from the thinker. The loose, leaning-back, breathing-out, smiling, keenly attentive, confident, unrushed presence blasts lucid ideas out of otherwise impenetrable vaults of confusion and doubt.

Ease is a deceptively gentle catalyst. Ease creates. Urgency destroys.

If you have spent most of your life with your heart racing and adrenaline running your days and ruining your nights, if one knee goes up and down when you are being 'still', or your heels and ankles flap back and forth when they are wrapped around each other under the table, if you wash dishes with your bottom sticking out on its way to somewhere else, if you write letters while you are on the phone, if you look at your watch while listening to someone and believe, really believe, that they don't notice, you will probably theorize against ease. If you can, you may even create policy to prevent it, just like the chief executive at lunch that day.

I suspect that the ease threshold in most executive pools is low. It is from this deficiency that people interrupt as a ritual of power. It is from this profound discomfort with the moment, with the self, with the easy beat of life as it actually is, that can make whole organizations seem, as Sara Hart of Hartcom put it, pathologically incapable of listening.

In this society ease is not easy. At least if we are hurrying, we can be seen to be doing something. And doing something is what produces results, isn't it? Not always. Most of the time being, with no rush, is what produces results. Sometimes, and particularly when it comes to helping someone think, doing requires not doing. To pay attention with a heart and mind at ease is what produces results. It is also – and this is almost impossible to remember – what produces time. A case study in London showed that a senior management team achieved time savings of 62 per cent when they ran their team as a Thinking Environment. That translated into 2,304 manager hours per year.

When it comes to thinking, the thing on which everything else depends, ease, that giant unattainable tiny thing, actually generates time we don't have if we rush.

Shirley Wardell, president of Evolve UK, said that thinking clearly and for yourself is the thing on which everything else depends. That sentence slithers right by you if you aren't looking. Ignored, it is deadly. So do notice. Because, if thinking clearly is the thing on which everything else depends, it is dangerous to keep doing the things that stop it. And it is indisputably intelligent, as well as astute, to do the things that help it along.

Ease recedes easily. But it is always retrievable. It is forgiving. And coming back to ease is inevitably the right thing to do.

CHAPTER 8

Encouragement

> Competition stifles encouragement
> and limits thinking.
>
> To be 'better than'
> is not necessarily to be good.

It is one thing to ask you to cultivate ease, to enjoy quiet, to communicate respect, to stop interrupting and let people finish, to give equal turns even in hierarchy, to help others do their *own* thinking. These I realize may seem iconoclastic enough. But there is just one more small thing. Well, actually, not so small. OK, true, it is possibly the most singularly worshipped centrepiece of industrialized society. But to examine it just might improve the quality of thinking beyond anything achieved in the past 200 years.

Consider the possibility that competition is not all it's cracked up to be.

Competition? The driving force behind capitalism and sport and technical progress? I know. But think about it this way. Competition between people ensures only one thing: that if you win, you will have done a *better* job at whatever it is than the other person did. That does not mean that you will have done a *good* job, just a better one. To compete does not ensure certain excellence. It just ensures comparative success. And the problem with that is that it distracts us from examining what good might actually be.

Just because you have written a better report than Richard does not mean you have written a good report. Just because you have won more court cases than Allyson does not mean you have served justice well. Just because your company has created a safer drug than the competition does not mean that you have protected the public. To have more customers than, to earn more money than, to make better grades than, to do 'more anything than' does not mean that what you are doing in the first place is good. Until we can let go of having to compete, it will be nearly impossible to ask the question, 'What would good be?'

Competition Kills Encouragement

Competition in a Thinking Environment is particularly hazardous. Competition between thinkers fractures your fortitude to ask the questions nobody wants asked. It keeps your attention on the rival, not on what you really think.

A Thinking Environment sets up a wholehearted, unthreatened search for good ideas. In order for a person to be able to think that well, with that much freshness and mettle, they have to be *encouraged* by the listener without smelling a bead of envy or competition from them. In a Thinking Environment encouragement is magic.

But if you as the listener feel competitive with the thinker, you cannot communicate this level of encouragement. Competing with the thinker, you may do any number of things to prevent them from being brilliant. You may steer them away from good ideas by suggesting they concentrate somewhere else, or by failing to listen well, caught up as you are in your own jealousy of the potential praise the thinker might receive for their good ideas. As a competitive listener you may curl your lip or shake your head or just look away in order to hold the person back from bright ideas.

Conversely, if the person thinking is competing with you, trying to seem more creative or clever than you, they will not be able to pursue their own ideas fully or honestly. They will be drawn back from the edge of an idea for fear it will not impress you. Competition of that sort will discourage their thinking *for themselves*.

A competitive listener is a thinking inhibitor. In fact 'competitive listener' is a serious oxymoron.

Try listening to someone next time without a shred of competition. Champion that person as a thinker. Be selflessly thrilled with the quality of their ideas. See what that feels like. Expect the same non-competitive attention from them in return for your thinking.

When competition between people drops away, everyone can reach for the stars. It is safe finally to venture out, even to dream again.

When people are not competing with each other to be best, it is possible to think all the way to something good.

CHAPTER 9

Feelings

Crying can make you smarter.

The human mind was designed to get intelligence back when it slips away. Can you believe a society would teach people to interfere with this mechanism the minute it starts? But this is exactly what we do, and we teach our children to do it too.

Thinking stops when we are upset. But if we express feelings just enough, thinking re-starts. Unfortunately, we have got this backwards in our society. We think that when feelings start, thinking stops. And so when crying starts, for example, we stop it. When we do this, we interfere with exactly the thing that helps a person to think clearly again.

One seriously flawed piece of handed-down 'wisdom' is the idea that when you start to cry you are out of control, falling apart, sick, going over the edge (whatever that is) and should do just about anything to 'pull yourself together'.

Also outrageous is the list of things we are encouraged to do to 'pull ourselves together'. We are sent off to isolate ourselves and repress; we are encouraged to put alcohol into our livers, or pour caffeine into our hearts; we are given nicotine to fill our lungs, or ice cream and cookies or ground cow muscle and deep-fried potatoes to fill our guts. These are all supposed to be fine. Crying, on the other hand – a genetically coded, wholly natural and intended means to rid the body of pain and toxicity – is not supposed to be fine.

Where did we go wrong?

We did not apply the same non-logic to any other natural release. We even have special rooms and designer decor and fragrant tissues for them. Perhaps we need feelings parlours, too, available whenever we are bombarded by pain and want a private environment in which to be embraced.

Not a chance. Our society is terrified of tears, and of anger and fear. We have mixed up the release of pain with the cause of pain. Stop crying and you'll stop hurting. Stop showing your anger and you'll stop being angry. Stop shaking and you'll stop being afraid. Just stop it.

It doesn't work. It never has. And not only does it not work – that is, stopping the release does not stop the pain (the pain just 'goes underground' and causes all sorts of neuroses and probably physical disease) – but, most important, repression of feeling represses clear thinking. It muddles the mind.

You see it every day. Someone is sad and needs to cry because they can't think. Someone is angry and needs to say so for a few minutes because they can't think. Someone is frightened and needs to talk about it and probably shake for a few minutes because they can't think. All around you every day are people whose churned-up, built-up feelings are blocking their thinking. But for some reason we make them stuff all those feelings back inside on pain of social death and then expect them to think and perform like geniuses. Even though, day after day, we can see right in our faces that this does not work, we do it over and over again.

If we would instead just let people cry, they would very soon think much better. If we would just sit with them, listen to them the way we would if they were talking, pay attention to them without panicking and without smothering them with our concern, they would recover in a very short time and be able to think for themselves again.

Watch what happens the next time someone cries in your presence, even if it is in the 'hallowed halls of professionalism' somewhere. Act as if it is perfectly natural and mature, which it is, and see how quickly the person begins to think again.

This is particularly important to do, and difficult, when someone is angry. Especially if they are angry with you. When they are angry, they are not thinking very well, so don't try to reason with them. Don't get in there with them as if they were logical at that moment. They are needing to say what is making them angry. Listen just the way you would listen to an interesting idea from them. Even try to get them to say more of the anger (of course, if they are actually violent, get out and negotiate another time in a setting that is safe for you) until it has truly subsided.

The positive effects of this are illustrated in the story about Dan the toxicologist (page 24). He was furious almost the minute his turn began, and everyone had to listen to him being angry. They could not interrupt or stop him. It worked. Within a very few minutes (few compared to the number of months they had been dealing with the non-thinking effects of their interruption and his unexpressed anger) he was thinking again and well. Suddenly, out of nowhere, he had the idea that he could get the product ready in three months. And everyone was relieved. I guarantee that if they had stopped him, shut him up in the middle of his anger as they usually did, he would not have had that life-saving (literally) idea. He would have withdrawn, sulked and cut off access to the good solution. His anger did not hurt anyone. His *repressed* anger was threatening millions.

It would be good to reduce this societal fear of feelings. And we really should start this change with our children. Childhood is where this brutal binding begins.

Recently I was just sitting on my deck across the road from a city playground. I was reading in the sun. After about twenty minutes eight children and three young mothers rolled up the long walk next to the playground and squeezed into the gates. Then the children, like jelly beans emptied out of a bag, tumbled down the walk towards the play area. Within seconds they zoomed towards the monkey bars, bounced on to the sand and with feet and hands climbed the steps to the slide and threw open their arms as they slid, giggling when they came with a thud back to earth.

Their happy screeching caught my ears. I looked up from my book. I remembered for an instant that clean quality of delight that humans are designed for. I smiled, felt the sun on my face and turned the page of my book.

But within five minutes one of the little boys began to cry. I looked up again. I spotted him. He toddled in teensy steps over to one of the mothers and screamed through his tears. She grabbed his arm, yelling at him to stop crying. He cried harder. She yelled louder.

She then dragged him away as he screamed and dropped him on to the concrete saying, 'Stay there until you stop crying.' She walked away. He ran after her with his arms outstretched, crying and screaming more.

She jerked him up and hit his bottom four times and yelled, 'Stop it! Now!' He didn't. And she hit him again. She then moved him like a football under her arm to a corner between the buildings and told him to stay there until he could stop being bad (that is, stop crying). She walked away, tossing her head in fury.

He ran after her, crying. She stopped, turned around and stamped her foot. She pointed her finger at him and yelled, 'No! You stay there until you've stopped making a scene.' She pointed again and he moved more slowly. 'Will you stop now? Will you?' he nodded and whimpered and tried to catch her steps as she moved on.

They both reached the other children and he blurted crying noises in single chords, gasping and then blurting again. She ran her fingers through her long hair, heaving it off her forehead, perhaps wondering what she had ever done to deserve this 'wilful' child and feeling furious and a failure all at once.

He managed finally to swallow and gasp and breathe out enough to cut off the crying and become acceptable to her. I couldn't stand to watch it any more and went inside.

I wonder why it is that human society makes everything so complicated. Why is it so hard for us to listen to a child cry until they can tell us what is wrong and we can help them think about how to solve it? Listening is simple.

Do we not do it because it seems to take too long? Do we think that we have lost control over the situation if we listen too long? Perhaps. But what we do instead can lead to truly out-of-control violence. And that takes a lot longer. It takes longer at the time and longer for years afterwards.

When people are trying to think for themselves, they just occasionally might cry or get angry or say they are frightened. Do not stop them. Be with them. Pay respectful attention to them. Hand them a tissue (soft and fragrant if possible). They will stop, sooner rather than later. And then they will think more clearly.

Improved thinking and behaviour are worth our listening through the feelings. And it does, I promise you, save time.

CHAPTER 10

Information, Sometimes

> The Thinker needs information –
> at the right moments.

That information is power is never more true than when you want people to think well. If ideas are based on error, the action that follows won't work. Facts, figures, concepts, directions, interpretations, policy – it doesn't matter; any information composing an accurate picture of reality is crucial to clear thinking on any subject. Withholding information from someone is an act of intellectual imperialism. Not bothering to seek accurate information is an act of intellectual recklessness.

Giving Information

Valuing information is easy. Supplying it in a Thinking Environment, however, is another story. When and how do you give information and not destroy the Thinking Environment for the person in the process?

Minimally, let the person speaking finish their sentence. Don't dump the correct information into the middle of it. People think better about new information if they don't feel assaulted just before the information is offered. And interruption is an assault on the thinking process.

Sam came distraught to Claire's office and said, 'How are we ever going to do Angie's work between the time she leaves and the time her replacement comes? Everyone is fed up because they are already working two hours a day longer than their contract says and feel resentful enough.'

Claire had just that morning found out that Angie's replacement was going to arrive a week *before* Angie would leave. That information, she knew, would completely eliminate Sam's concern. It was tempting to stop him right in the middle of his first sentence, when she first heard his error, and set him straight. But she let him finish. Because she waited, two good things happened. For one, he felt dignified for having not been knocked down by the interruption. He thought better about the information because of that dignity. Also Sam spontaneously gave his boss information on an issue that would not have had a chance to appear if she had stopped him. The near fury the staff was feeling about their work load in general needed attention. It was good that he said that and that Claire heard it.

Supply information, of course. But time it so that it keeps a Thinking Environment strong between you. Ask yourself, 'When and how do I do this so that this person can keep thinking well?

Bad Motives

Notice that the second you realize there is misinformation, however minuscule, however tangential, bobbing in and out of the person's thoughts, the temptation can be overwhelming to stop them and supply it. This sudden craving to correct them emerges usually when your *discomfort* at being there, at ease, giving attention is eating you alive. This urge grabs you because you sense that finally you will have something 'active' to do. It feels good. Beware of this zing.

Also, don't give information to show off. Ask yourself, 'Why am I choosing to give this information now? Is it so that I will look on the ball? Or is it truly to help the person think better?'

Supply information only when you are sure that it will make a decisive difference in the direction, content or progress of the person's thinking.

Asking for Information

Similarly, *asking* for information *from* the Thinker needs to be timed well.

Following this principle I have a few times listened to people without interruption even when I had a completely wrong idea of what they were talking about. On one occasion I was conducting a team development programme in a pharmaceutical company. I was demonstrating how to give the kind of attention that helps people think fast, clearly and imaginatively. The team listened along with me. Holly began.

'I want to figure out what to say to the development committee about this candidate.'

I pictured a job applicant.

'We have been working with this candidate for nearly two years.'

That's a long time to spend recruiting just one person, I thought. Expensive too. Must be important.

'I think we are ready to recommend advancement into the next level of development.'

Another stage of interviews? How did they ever get 30,000 people hired around here?

'But there are some problems.' Holly went on for another five minutes. She thought of one idea after another, each feeding the next. She was unequivocally on a roll. She even once stopped and said to me how grateful she was finally to be able to think this through. More connections and a few more ideas poured out of her. The others on the team were alert and not the least bit confused. I, however, still wondered how much older that applicant would be by the time he got the job.

'The problem I can now see is not so much with the candidate. It has every chance of being a successful compound. The problem is with the committee leader.'

Compound. Right. The candidate is a drug. Got it.

I was glad I had not asked her to explain to me their bizarre employee recruitment policies or why this person had all the time in the world to be hired. I was glad, not because I would have revealed my ignorance, which is never fun. I was glad because my requests for information would have stopped her and been of no help to her whatsoever. I was glad I had observed her closely enough to notice that she was thinking for herself beautifully second by second even without my complete understanding. The request for information would have been a jarring deflection of attention on to me.

Holly finished her turn with two new ideas about how to handle the committee leader. Everyone was impressed.

Asking for information should occur only if it is necessary for the person thinking to think well. And the question should be asked only when it will not interupt a successful stream of thought.

Holly's session was not the most outrageous example of the principle of inserting or asking for information strategically. I even listened once to a woman who spoke for fifteen minutes in Italian, not a language I know. She said she was sure she could find out what she really thought about the issue on her mind if she could talk about it first in her native language, with my respectful attention. The adventurer in me said yes and she was off. She seemed pleased with what she had accomplished while my listening was enough. When she then needed questions from me to help her remove assumptions, she had to switch to English and do a quick summary job for me, but it worked.

Information can be important or it can be superfluous. You can become expert at discerning which is which. The more you begin to enjoy paying attention and being still, *inside* yourself, the easier that discernment will be.

Denial

By information I mean not just the supplying of technically correct information, but also the piercing of denial.

Denial is the assumption that what is true is not true. When something, for whatever reason, is too difficult to face, your mind can interpret it as something else. A colleague humiliates you in a meeting, more than once. Everyone around the table winces, but no one speaks. No one, including you, stops it. Almost immediately your mind interprets her behaviour as an aberrant outburst, then as 'the way powerful people behave' and then as nothing to make a fuss about. By the next day you have began to think it didn't actually happen. Sure, she got a little annoyed, but nothing dramatic happened, did it?

This is denial. It is the antithesis of reality. It is dangerous because thinking works best in the presence of reality. Part of reality is correct information about what is real, even if what is real is very painful or disappointing or threatening. Your mind does have the capacity to handle anything. But it can't do it if you present it with lies.

Questions help to puncture denial. A few powerful ones are:

- What is in my face that I am not facing?
- What is the worst thing that can happen if I face this? What is the worst thing that can happen if I don't?
- What am I assuming that makes me turn away from this?

There is another good question we can ask that pierces denial. I call it the Amy Question because my dear friend Amy thought it up. It acknowledges the phenomenon of our being willing to deny difficulties at the beginning of something because we prefer a romanticized pastel view of what is ahead. But in fact if we ask the Amy Question early enough, and then face the answer, we can prevent heartache and failure which otherwise can trip us up because we lived too long in denial.

What startled me about it the first time she asked me was her astute recognition that we can usually go for about a year before we are forced to see what had been right in our face from the beginning. The Amy Question is: 'What do you already know that you are going to find out in a year?' This question requires you to supply and face your *own* information. Ask it at the beginning of any relationship or enterprise or change.

Accurate, complete information is vital if people are going to think for themselves, clearly and boldly. So give information and ask for it – but only at the right times.

CHAPTER 11

Place

A Thinking Environment
says back to you,
'You matter.'

We used to have student conferences in the boiler room next to our classroom. It was the only available space at the time. In that room were a washing machine, a dryer and two huge furnaces. It wasn't called the boiler room for nothing. The walls were cinder block and grey. The floor was concrete. Pipes ran across the ceiling, bypassing the single light bulb whose string dangled and swung when our heads hit it before we sat down. We sat on two metal chairs.

It did not take me too many weeks to notice that when students went into the boiler room to talk about a problem, they did not always emerge thinking better. At first I thought this was because we were occasionally interrupted by a faculty member putting laundry in the dryer and heating the place until we were scorching. Finally, it occurred to me that perhaps the room itself was the problem. Possibly it was not the ideal environment for thinking well and feeling better. The fact that it was private did not seem to compensate for the grey cinder-block effect.

So I filled the room with orange. I put up orange chenille bed spreads on the walls. I put orange cushions on the chairs and artificial zinnias on top of the dryer. My efforts still did not seem to encourage a positive attitude among the students. However, there wasn't much to be done about this until spring when we could meet on two chairs outside under the trees. So we made do.

In later years, when we were systematically searching for the components of a Thinking Environment, I stumbled on to this boiler room thing and thought about it some more. I began by assuming that for a physical space to be conducive to fresh thinking it needed to be the exact opposite of a boiler room – big, with windows all around and things of nature everywhere like real plants, and a view of the sky. I guessed it needed to be tidy and pretty and perhaps even elegant. And definitely not scorching.

Then I did some work for a major British bank and was 'treated' to its headquarters in the City of London. That multi-million-pound building was sleek, big, with windows everywhere, huge plants, the perfect temperature and miles of carpet and designer furniture. But I don't think I have ever been so immediately stifled in an environment in my life. It was no better than the boiler room had been.

I realized that appearance is not the key. I began to wonder what two such differently designed and furnished places could have in common. Both had made it hard to think. I asked myself the question, 'What was I assuming while in those two environments that stopped me from thinking well?' The answer surprised me: 'I don't matter here.'

Since then I have found consistently that Thinking Environments are places that simply say back to the people, 'You matter.' When that is the guideline for architectural design and decoration, very different places emerge than when some abstract standard of opulence and furnishing is the guide or when pure functionality is the standard.

I was intrigued to read about an advertising agency in London called St Luke's. Juliet Soskice, marketing manager, describes the place as 'the antithesis of an ad agency'. The office space is friendly, full of bright colours and natural light, possibly even more relaxing than the employees' homes, with a restaurant in the basement and a room next door specifically for pregnant women to relax. There is an area called the 'cool stuff' room and a Boots No. 7 room which has space for work at computer terminals, a bed above for thinking and de-stressing and other desks with comfortable chairs. Juliet says she is 'passionate about it' (*The Times Magazine*, 18 April 1998, Anna Blundy). The people who work there have designed it to reflect their own spirit. The place also expresses the non-hierarchical business structure, the equality among the work force and the respect people have for each other.

A different and very striking example of place saying 'You matter' is the London Lighthouse. The architects were chosen because they had no design plans when they arrived for the bidding interview. They said that their strategy would be to talk with people with HIV and with others who would be using the service and find out what they needed and wanted in the building. They said they would design the renovations to make it clear that the people who used the building were what mattered.

And they did it. The building, with its curved entrance, opens its arms to the whole community. The colours, mostly terracotta, ash and blue, soften the light that streams in from the sky lights and windows. The reception desk is around to the side so that your first experience is not to be scrutinized, but to be at peace. A garden at the back off the spacious cafe seems nurturing in every leaf and blossom. There are wooden tables under brightly coloured umbrellas from many different cultures. Original art of many kinds, all contributed by people affected by the virus, clothe the walls. One man with AIDS actually said, 'The minute you walk in, this place gives you the unsettling sense that you matter profoundly.'

What would have to change about your work space (especially if you are 'hot desking'), or even your home, for it to say back to you, 'You matter'?

CHAPTER 12

Diversity

**Diversity raises
the intelligence of groups.**

**Homogeneity
is a form of denial.**

Diversity enhances thinking because it is true.

The world *is* diverse. But because diversity, the differences between groups, is still the excuse for discrimination, disempowerment and even genocide, we have been taught to hate or to deny our differences rather than to welcome them. Our differences are real and good. And to think well about almost any topic, we need to be in as real, and therefore as diverse, a setting as possible.

The mind works best in the presence of reality. It spontaneously scours for facts. Conversely, the mind seems to lose its edge when having to work in pretence, denial, or fabrication. And homogeneity, when you think about it, is a form of denial. It is a form of pretence. To say, by your group composition, that the world is all the same is a lie.

Most of the decisions affecting the largest number of people in our society are made by homogeneous groups. Even today the closer to the top you go, the whiter, more male, more heterosexual, more middle-aged and middle-class the group looks. And it won't do to cite the one blind, homeless, working-class lesbian in a wheelchair you recruited for your board. Tokenism is also denial.

Diversity, on the other hand, is the truth. It is a thinking enhancer because it frees the mind of two sorts of limiting assumptions:

- that the dominant group is superior and so everyone should be (think) like them;
- that because the dominant group is superior it should have power over the others.

Real diversity is achieved when groups are stripped of both of those assumptions, when differences are celebrated and when power lies in the hands of a truly mixed group. When real diversity emerges, a Thinking Environment does too.

On the Thinking Environment course people make a list of all the groups they identify with that have been the brunt of societal prejudice or discrimination. Usually people can think of twenty or more. Diversity is the mixing of groups based on obvious identities such as race, gender, class, sexual orientation, region and income. But it also includes differences such as political identity, company department, fields of work, education, place in the hierarchy or even postal codes, sports club memberships and, when you are little, differences in what's in your lunch box. All of these group identities can become a basis for discrimination and can make people treat each other so badly they cannot think for themselves when they are with each other. (I am not kidding about the lunch boxes. Read the chapter on childhood prejudice in *Bird By Bird* by Anne Lamott.)

Participants write down the limiting assumptions the world makes about their groups. Then we construct an Incisive Question to remove each of those assumptions. This gives people insight into each other's real experience of battling internalized oppression. The question removes the assumption and gives them the power to think for themselves. For example, the limiting assumption about members of the working class might be: 'You are unworthy, lacking in social skills and stupid.' The Incisive Question to remove this assumption could be: 'If you and the world knew that you are the deserving foundation of society, graceful and intelligent, how would you walk through the world?'

The assumption made about *every* minority or disenfranchized group is: 'You can't think.' People outside the group believe this and spread the lie. People inside the group believe it and spread the lie. For this lie to be dispelled it will be necessary for decision-making groups to include as many people from marginalized groups as possible. The people outside the group will quickly see that 'those people' can think, and 'those people' will quickly see that they themselves and others like them *can* think.

Tricia is as clever and enterprising, as professionally expert as they come. But one day she had to write a proposal for a consulting contract her company wanted very much. She couldn't do it. Her fingers stalled on the keys with the first line. So she called me. 'Do you have ten minutes to listen to me think about this bloody proposal?'

'Sure.' I sat back.

'I just can't do this. Just listen to the question on this form: "What exactly do you expect the optimum outcomes to be of this project? How will it interface with already existing programmes? List the metrics by which you would test the validity of the outcomes and the qualifications of the experts administering them." That makes me unconscious.' She paused. 'I hate it,' she said. 'I can't think of anything to say even though I know the project thoroughly. I can't make my brain or my fingers move.'

I kept listening.

'I want to write this proposal this afternoon.' She paused and then said, 'That's it. What should I do?'

So I asked her, 'What might you be assuming that could be keeping you from writing the proposal this afternoon?'

'I am assuming that they will turn it down.'

I said, 'What else?'

'I am assuming that they will see me as just a working-class, Glaswegian, Catholic female and never give me a chance. That's the worst one.'

'They might,' I said, 'but what are you assuming that makes that possibility stop you from writing the proposal?'

'I am assuming that people like me aren't good enough and can't think.'

So I said, 'If you knew that working-class, Glaswegian, Catholic females are good enough and *can* think, what would you do to write the proposal this afternoon?'

'If I knew all those things, I would lighten up, get a cup of tea, sit back down and write what I know.'

'Good,' I said, 'I'll ask you again in case there are other ideas. If you knew that working-class, Glaswegian, Catholic females are good enough and *can* think, what else would you do to write the proposal this afternoon?'

'Well, for one thing I would feel a lot more interested in the whole thing and I would want to write the proposal honestly and with my own sort of flair. I wouldn't feel constrained by the stupid form. Oh,' she said, with a lilt in her voice, 'and I would stop apologizing every few seconds in my head. I would feel a bit proud and keep thinking about the contracts I have done that were successful. Yeah, I would keep my mind there and not on their tedious prejudices, if they even have them. How do I know what they think of Catholic, Glaswegian, working-class women anyway? And who the hell cares?'

Her voice had changed in less than ten minutes. We hung up. She did the proposal, finishing before dinner that evening. She said a few months later that she got two contracts out of that afternoon's work.

Sexism: The Particular Culprit

Sexism, like regionalism, homophobia, racism, classism – every bedrock assumption and norm of superiority – stops people from thinking for themselves. But sexism also has a particular price to pay for poor thinking in our society (for detail on this subject please see my book *Women and Power: How Far Can We Go?* BBC Worldwide).

Sexism, the set of assumptions saying that men and men's culture are superior to women and women's culture, contains specific instructions *not to build a Thinking Environment*. From the beginning of their life men are taught, in the name of their manhood, to divest their behaviour of all ten components of a Thinking Environment. They are not supposed to give quality attention to people. They are told to control, not to be at ease. They must criticize, not appreciate. They are not allowed to cry. Women, on the other hand, from the beginning of their life, and in the name of their womanhood, are allowed to retain Thinking Environment qualities.

Male-conditioned Leaders and a Thinking Environment

Because men (and a few women) carrying this conditioning have been historically the leaders and their conditioning the model for leadership, most of our organizations are not Thinking Environments. Look at how men's conditioning and a Thinking Environment vie:

Thinking Environment	Male Conditioning
Listen	Take over and talk
Ask Incisive Questions	Know everything
Establish equality	Assume superiority
Appreciate	Criticize
Be at ease	Control
Encourage	Compete
Feel	Toughen
Supply accurate information	Lie
Humanize the place	Conquer the place
Create diversity	Deride difference

It takes several years before boys complete the process of packing away and denying these ten very human parts of their nature. But with enough bullying, violent play, ridicule and absorption of the role models and myths about what real men are, boys eventually and in varying degrees succumb. This renunciation of Thinking Environment behaviour is a painful process. Some men have even likened it to torture.

The depth of this conditioning was chillingly clear on a course we ran called Young People as Leaders. We were exploring the assumptions the world still makes about men and boys and how those assumptions distort the way they behave with each other and thus how they shape their leadership. We were talking about the assumption that 'real men' take over and talk, that they do not easily settle in with someone and give them profound levels of attention.

'I don't think that's true,' said Mark. 'I give guys and other people attention. Like in the locker room after a game when we are discussing the plays that worked and stuff. And when we talk about girls and things. You know. We're good at giving attention.'

The other young men nodded. I heard a muffled chuckle from the young women. I said, 'You do give attention. But it is sometimes not the quality or breadth of attention required for a Thinking Environment. May I demonstrate what I mean?'

'Sure,' Mark said quickly, 'no problem.'

I asked Mark to sit across from Jim. I suggested that Mark just look at Jim.

He did. Then he looked back at me and said, 'OK, I did it; what's next?'

I said, 'Look at him again and this time notice him.'

He looked back as I had asked but looked away quickly. And he began to sweat. His hands began to shake. 'What do you want me to notice?' he asked me.

'Him,' I said.

'What do you mean, him?'

'Well, keep your eyes on his eyes, and tell me what you see.'

He looked back and then away and said, 'Nothing in particular. Just a guy sitting there. He's all right, I guess.'

'This time look at him a few seconds longer, and warmly.'

He winced. He looked into space.

'What are you thinking?' I asked.

'Nothing,' he replied.

I listened.

'I was thinking that what you asked me to do is just about the most disgusting thing I can imagine.'

The room became very still. Mark looked down at his hands.

'Then he flung his head back and said, 'I feel sick. I think this whole thing is disgusting. Completely. In fact, I don't even know what we are doing this for. It's stupid.'

He looked at the young women sitting near.

'OK, what the hell. This is no big deal.'

Mark looked at Jim, kept his eyes on Jim's eyes for a few seconds longer than before, squinted and turned up the corners of his mouth. Jim looked down and giggled.

'OK, I did it,' Mark said.

'No you didn't,' said Jim, surprising us. 'You looked like a dork. I'm not saying I could do this right either, but I sure wouldn't call what you did warm. Which, by the way, is just fine with me.'

'Try again?' I suggested calmly.

'Sure,' Mark said.

He looked down again. I thought about the seconds of complete composure a diver uses before executing a perfect dive. Mark looked up suddenly, stared at Jim for one second and then shook his head. He looked at me.

'Look,' he said, 'I understand that this shouldn't be hard, and that probably I should be able to do this, but I don't want to. I get along really fine the way I am. My life isn't all that bad – my grades are great; I am going to a top university next year; I am captain of the football and wrestling teams; I have a gorgeous girl friend; I feel good. If I were to get to the point where I could look at a guy like that, with that kind of attention for a long time, warmly and everything, I feel that the very cornerstone of my life would collapse, and I would be left with nothing.'

I memorized his words. They seemed incongruously sophisticated. They summed up precisely the horrors of male conditioning. Immobility: a cornerstone of a life. Disconnection: a non-negotiable base from which to do everything. The basis of leadership of the future? And yet one of the top young achievers in the country.

Everyone in the room was sweating. The young men were quiet. The women were incredulous. How could it be, they asked later, that just to look easily and warmly at another guy could be felt as foundation-threatening? To the women, whose culture had never forced them away from this ability, attention and warmth were natural, fine, indispensable.

Male conditioning ravages young lives in front of our eyes. If we were to decide to see it for what it is and not deny or romanticize it nor interpret it as genetically inevitable, we could stop it. This training of men to be real men by denouncing much good human behaviour is based on the assumption that these human characteristics are somehow female. And the key thing boys and men are told never to do is get themselves confused with a woman.

A recent *Times* article that revealed unemployment figures among boys in Britain stated that their unemployment stems from the successful employment and academic achievement of girls. It said that girls should *not* have the jobs if it means boys will be unemployed. Apparently boys become despondent, angry and then violent when their self-esteem drops because of unemployment or underachievement. The article also stated that boys will not seek most of the jobs girls have because the jobs are service or 'soft' jobs and boys think the jobs are not fit for a man.

Our job, it would seem to me, is not to get the girls out of the jobs but to get the male conditioning out of the boys.

I would like to see us stop the conditioning of boys in our lifetime.

Women Emulating Men

The inevitable thing about the messages of superiority is that the non-dominant group is taught to revere the very group that is marginalizing it. In particular it is encouraged to take on the dominant group's leadership behaviour. As a result, as more and more women have moved into positions of leadership, they have done so by adopting men's conditioning and espousing it as the best way to lead and to have influence. This is not progress. Women have been encouraged to 'be like men' when actually the best thing for men and society would be to encourage men to 'be like women'.

Men themselves tell me, when there are no other men within ear shot, that they don't much like the backstabbing, competitive, patronizing, exclusive, interruptive environments of their meetings and organizations either. And research shows that if they don't get out of these environments in time, or change them, many men eventually die from them.

What society needs, I believe, is an environment that has the best of both women's and men's cultures and discards the conditioning of both. In such an environment people will be confident and humble, outspoken and quiet, logical and spontaneous, decisive and flexible, and always inclusive and respectful. The environment will laud neither the deferential, ditsy-conditioned female nor the controlling, competitive-conditioned male. What society needs is the whole human being, where gender matters only if you are trying to put together a baby and is irrelevant if you are trying to put together an effective organization. The best of women's and men's cultures will ensure the building of Thinking Environments in our institutions.

Your Own Prejudices

The embedded prejudice about thinking that arrives with us into adult-hood can steal into every interaction and must be watched. The minute you begin listening to someone, your assumption about their ability to think for themselves will affect how well you pay attention and how confident you are in the likelihood that they will think perhaps even better than you can about their issue. If you think their brain is inferior to yours, they will know it even if you do a dance a minute trying to hide it.

It is probably a good idea to lay out in front of yourself the assumptions of inferiority of intellect you may harbour. Even if you admit it only to yourself. There is no need to feel bad or guilty about these assumptions. They jumped on your back when you were very young and weren't looking and are some of the unexamined assumptions you have carried around every since.

Look at them. And then ask yourself a question like this: If I knew that the people who I have been taught are less intelligent than I am are actually bright and able to think well about any subject of their choice, how would I feel and behave during their Thinking Session? And how would I regard them as my listener during my turn to think?

The human mind wants the truth. It wants to be fed with the diversity that nature spun into the human design. Welcoming our differences, reclaiming our right to every positive human quality is not only politically correct and decent; it is essential if human thinking is to advance.

CHAPTER 13

What About Solitude?

Until we are distracted,
solitude is a Thinking Environment.

I sometimes feel we might benefit from official areas in our work places designated exclusively for quiet time alone to think – sanctuaries for the human mind. Surely if we can pay millions for gyms and cafes and auditoriums, we can budget and build a thinking space. But regardless, people find productive thinking time in solitude wherever they can – on walks, in the bath and behind the windows of rush hour. Solitude is a human requirement. For many of us solitude is the only place where we are not attacked or belittled or overtaken. It is the best Thinking Environment because it does not re-enforce the limiting assumptions that make us think we cannot think.

However, in solitude we are easily distracted by the laneless traffic of other issues in our brain that screech for our attention. In fact, we can be so distracted, meandering off into tangential climes, that we don't for several minutes (or even days) realize we have failed to think all the way through the original idea. Solitude can be sustained as a Thinking Environment only as long as we don't interrupt ourselves with these distractions and, most important, as long as we are not wrapped unawares in limiting assumptions. It is then that the benefit of attention, Incisive Questions and focused encouragement from a human thinking partner become obvious. Solitude and attention are different routes to good thinking. We need them both.

Part Two

Creating a Thinking Environment

I. The Thinking Organization

CHAPTER 14

The Thinking Team

A Thinking Environment
is the core of team effectiveness.

The Power of the Group

Every minute, even while you sleep, groups known as organizations are meeting to decide how you will live. They are deciding whether you will work or not; whether you will suffer or luxuriate; what you will be allowed to know and when; where you should put your faith; what you will put into your body; and how much all of this will cost. These groups are deciding who matters and how much. In fact, most of what affects each of our minute-to-minute individual lives is decided by groups meeting without us. We have to trust them. And when *we* are in one of those organizations making some of those decisions, we have to be trusted.

But just how good can the thinking of these groups be? Only as good – as accurate, as sound, as generous, as imaginative, as dignifying – as the way group members treat each other while they think. Their decisions will be as good as their thinking; their thinking will be as good as the number of Thinking Environment components present when they meet. Fortunately human beings were designed to provide each other with exactly these conditions.

Over the centuries, however, societies, in the name of advancement, in order to conquer and rule, have stripped themselves of each of these thinking conditions, one by one. They have systematically eliminated a Thinking Environment from our world.

Yet we can retrieve it. Groups in organizations can be taught to master all ten components of a Thinking Environment and to use them together. Time after time, when groups operate this way, the results are impressive. Groups produce better ideas in less time at less cost and with higher spirits. The effects on organizations of operating in a Thinking Environment justify optimism, even at this late and wobbly date in human history. But inside the organization we have to be willing to behave differently. The most strategic place to begin this organizational change is in the management of teams.

Managing the Thinking Team

Teams are now the primary force of organizations. They are worth cultivating at their core. Their core is the *mind* of each team member.

Team effectiveness depends on the calibre of thinking the team can do. When teams know how to meet as a Thinking Environment and how to exchange ideas one to one in this way, when they know how, in other words, to keep each other thinking all the time, they perform at increasingly high levels.

Managers of high-performing teams have to be masters of the oxymoron: securing change, committing to uncertainty and requiring autonomy. Formulae and habit won't do; only thinking will.

In every manager's training programme, in every MBA curriculum, the theory and process of a Thinking Environment should be fundamental. The future of work depends on it.

The most powerful vehicle for team thinking is the team meeting. A manager's ability to turn meetings into a Thinking Environment is probably an organization's greatest asset. Managers who run meetings in this way are virtually certain to raise the quality of the team's performance. Knowing how to manage a thinking team is fundamental to building tomorrow's successful organization. The following chapters will look at this in some depth.

CHAPTER 15

Meeting This Way

Giving everyone a turn
increases the intelligence of groups.

Knowing they won't be interrupted
frees people to think faster and say less.

Meetings are where the heart of an organization beats. Organizational life flows from there.

Some people literally spend all day in meetings. Considering the quality of most of those meetings, it is a wonder that all managers and executives have brains left at the end of the day. Perhaps you think they don't. Some of the policies and products that they market with a straight face can certainly make you wonder.

A meeting run as a Thinking Environment is different. It produces better ideas in less time, provides the participants with the courage to act and leaves the group feeling good about itself. That may sound impossible, but I have seen it hundreds of times.

Chairing Brilliant Meetings

If you want people to say of your meetings that 'they just don't get better than this', chair them as a Thinking Environment. As team leader or manager or chair of a meeting, consider following these nine simple guidelines:

At the beginning:
1 Give *everyone a turn* to speak.

2 Ask everyone to say what is *going well* in their work, or in the group's work.

Throughout:

3 Give attention *without interruption* during open and even fiery discussion.
4 Ask Incisive Questions to reveal and *remove assumptions* that are limiting ideas.
5 Divide into *Thinking Partnerships* when thinking stalls and give each person five minutes to think out loud without interruption.
6 Go around intermittently to give everyone a turn to say what they think.
7 Permit also the sharing of truth and *information*.
8 Permit the expression of *feelings*.

At the end:

9 Ask everyone what they thought went well in the meeting and what they respect in each other.

When you are bold enough to do even *one* of these things, the quality of thinking in the meeting rises. Meetings with all nine guidelines in place have been described by some participants as superb.

Dan's meeting (Chapter 1) was an example of this structure's potential to save lives. The structure also has the potential to save talent, as Leo discovered.

Throw Me Under a Bus

Leo was a rebel. He wanted the people in his team to think for themselves. They resisted. They said he should be more directive, that he was a weak leader. They were used to javelin-throwing control addicts and they dreaded Leo's wimpy meetings. Nothing seemed to happen in those meetings. No fur flew. No whips cracked. Leo was waiting for *them* to take responsibility.

But even Leo admitted his strategy wasn't working well. Just not to dominate didn't seem to be the answer. Some other sort of leadership was needed.

Then he tried running the meetings as a Thinking Environment. At the next meeting, he began with the opening positive rounds and, although they did not feel like it particularly, the team complied. At least, they thought, it was different.

Leo presented the first agenda item. 'We want more women in our company. We spend millions every year trying to recruit the best and the brightest female engineers from university. We attract a few, but for some reason we lose many more. They take a look at our company and go elsewhere.

'The women we do get are the tops. We spend millions training and supporting them along with the new male recruits. But after two years many of the women leave.

'And, of course, we lose the talent of those we have trained as well as the money we have invested in them. No one wins.

'We have to come up with successful ways to attract and keep female graduates. Before we open for general discussion, I'll go around the group first to get each of your ideas on this question: How can we change the way we recruit and manage women so that we do not lose them? Neal, will you be first?'

This was strange. Leo had never been this directive, this systematic and yet he was still asking people to take responsibility for their own ideas. This combination intrigued them. Everyone spoke. The ideas were interesting.

Then he opened the discussion. He told people anyone could speak but that no one could interrupt. 'If you get too long-winded, I'll stop you. Two minutes is about long enough.'

A discussion fired up. But the ideas did not yet seem good enough to Leo.

So he asked, 'What are we assuming that could be limiting our ideas here?'

He broke the group of sixteen into pairs and gave each person five minutes to think with attention and no interruption about that question. When they came back to the circle, Leo put some of their answers on the flip chart:

- This is Leo's problem, not ours.
- What we say won't be implemented anyway.
- The leaders of this department should work this out among themselves.
- The team must wait for the people in charge to decide.
- I don't know enough to think about this.

'These are all assumptions of your powerlessness,' he said. 'No matter what I say you seem to throw the ball back to me. But I want you to take charge here. I want your ideas.

'I'll ask you the following question and then we'll go around and get everyone's ideas.'

On the chart he wrote: 'If all the current leaders of this department were to fall under a bus, and you were appointed leader, what would be the first thing you would do to recruit and keep female engineers?'

One at a time high-calibre ideas peeked out from that group. One idea in particular stunned everyone because it was blindingly simple *and* consistent with Leo's passion for empowerment. It was the kind of idea, in fact, that embarrasses because it should have been policy ages ago.

'The first thing I would do is ask the women themselves,' Serena said. 'Ask the recruits that turn us down and ask the women who leave. Then do what they suggest.'

Ask them. Still a radical idea.

They did. The report from the interviews with the women recruits and employees gave that company irrefutable insight into some of what it needed to change. One collection of suggestions included these:

- Cut out the games-playing you do with each other.
- Say 'I am sorry' and 'I don't know' rather than waffling to protect yourselves from looking stupid.
- Eliminate the pecking order of higher grades/better cars/larger windows.
- Define a job by the work that needs doing, not by the time spent in the office.
- Acknowledge when and who says something. Don't pinch ideas and then take the credit. Give credit properly and generously.
- Set up peer mentoring to share experiences and to find the heart to keep going when under attack and pressure.
- Sweep the road or sit with the Queen of England – do whatever needs to be done.
- Share the good things that people and teams have achieved.
- Be direct.
- Treat people as human beings – be interested in their real life, not just in their work. Help them solve the balancing act. Don't deny it or punish women for it: it is real.
- Be imaginative in the early shortlisting. Include women whose background does not always literally fulfil the requirements.
- Take risks with energetic, intelligent women.
- Give people clarity and autonomy, space and support.
- Praise people.
- Listen.

Leo's next meeting recorded in its minutes, 'The process of asking each woman why she did not choose the company or why she left it has led us to consider a company-wide diversity and culture change campaign.'

Leo's team operates as a Thinking Environment most of the time now. He likes it that the team members more readily accept their power. They like it that he leads more decisively. They all like the quality of the thinking that is beginning to seem commonplace.

Embedded in Leo's meeting were the nine meeting guidelines (pages 102–3) which contain the ten components of a Thinking Environment. Each one is important and contributes to the gathering power of good ideas.

1 Give everyone a turn

Most important of the meeting guidelines is that everyone has a turn to speak, several times, knowing they will not be interrupted. The other eight aspects of a thinking meeting are vital, but this feature alone improves the quality of thinking in the group dramatically.

2 Begin with positive reality

If you don't do anything else, just try this: open your meeting by going around the group systematically twice to give everyone a turn to speak:

a) Let the first round be a *positive* reflection on people's work or the work of the project. People think better throughout the whole meeting if the very first thing they do is to say something true and positive about how their work or the work of the group is going. The mind responds best to a full picture of reality. And always a huge part of reality is what is good.

Most of a group's focus when they enter a meeting is on what is not going well. To provide a full picture of reality it is necessary to get people from the beginning to articulate what is truly going well. Focusing on the positive first sets up better thinking conditions for dealing later with the problems.

But make sure the question is not mushy or superficial. And that you are not either. People resist gush, especially at work. Three good questions are: 'What is going well in your work or life?', 'What successes have you had since we last met?' and 'What do you think is going well in our project?'

This positive assessment of work, a blending of accurate thought and honesty of the heart is not touchy/feely. It is rigorous and professional – and a vital piece of good group thinking.

b) Let the second round be ideas about the first agenda item. State the agenda item clearly. Then go round the group to get each person's ideas. Be clear that no one speaks again until everyone has had a turn. Prevent these systematic go-rounds from turning prematurely into a discussion. Open discussion comes afterwards and will then be more intelligent. If you *begin* by giving everyone a turn in sequence this way, the chances increase that the quiet people will speak again during the open discussion. This increases the number and quality of ideas generated throughout the meeting. It also means that at the end of the meeting there will be greater co-operation with any decision the group or chair makes.

3 Let them finish

In groups talkative people adore interrupting. They like to know that whenever they get the urge, they can blitz their way into whoever's sentence happens to be walking innocently across the group at that moment.

Interrupting is touted as a strong, assertive, intelligent thing to do, but in fact it is none of these. It is actually an assault on the thinking process and is selfish and costly. Ideas are crushed in the wake of interruption and policies are developed that are based on immature fragments of ideas.

So prevent it. Get everyone to agree not to interrupt each other.

In a Thinking Environment you *will* have your turn. That is the good thing about this process: everyone gets a turn and no one gets trampled. And while you wait, you'll begin to understand why it is that the quiet people, listening so long, sometimes have the best ideas.

You can exchange ideas; you can disagree; you can fight; you can joke; you can create all kinds of synergy. Just don't interrupt. Discuss freely, but let each other finish. When people know they will have a turn and be allowed to finish their thought, they think more quickly and say less. When they anticipate interruption, on the other hand, they grasp for edges of ideas, they rush; and they elaborate. Interruption takes up more time than allowing people to sweep cleanly through to the end of an idea.

If you are worried about all of this taking too much time, remember: giving everyone time saves time.

4 Identify assumptions and ask Incisive Questions

People go into a meeting assuming several limiting things. One is that their ideas don't matter, that they cannot add value to the meeting. Another assumption is that to think for themselves and to say what they think will displease the leader and jeopardize their job.

Another is that other people there are more important than they are; or, conversely, that they are the most important person there and that the best use they can make of the meeting is to silence others and impress.

A Thinking Environment, by its very structure, removes those assumptions. It replaces them with freeing assumptions like 'Your ideas do matter; what you think can add value to this meeting; you are as important as any other person here; your job is best done by contributing your thinking to the meeting; and you will impress people best if you encourage them, draw them out, and offer your knowledge only if it clearly is needed.'

Those freeing assumptions, implicit in the rounds of equal turns, in the freedom from interruption, in the periods of positive assessment and in the opportunity to find and remove other limiting assumptions, lead to far better ideas than are possible in other meeting structures.

The structure of a Thinking Environment meeting in itself removes most limiting assumptions from people's thinking. But other, more work-endemic assumptions will not necessarily be budged just by the structure of the meeting. To remove these assumptions the group needs Incisive Questions. I suggest people post the following in front of the meeting each time:

- What might we be assuming that could be limiting our thinking here?
- If we assumed something more freeing, what new ideas might we have?

5 Divide into thinking pairs

When ideas are flagging or when the group needs to remove limiting assumptions by asking Incisive Questions, try this: divide the group into pairs and give each person five minutes to think uninterrupted for themselves with a partner's undivided, respectful attention. Inevitably this Thinking Partnership structure re-ignites thinking. It also re-energizes the group.

6 Go round again

At several points, including after Thinking Partnerships, do another round of the group. Give everyone a turn to speak again without interruption. You will be surprised and pleased at how productive this very, very simple process is.

In fact, it is very often right here, in the go-round following discussion, that time is saved, that a new idea that solves everything emerges. It will seem as if it will be too time-consuming to go round again. You will want to resist doing it, but do it anyway, because it is exactly in this process of hearing from *everyone* that something almost magical happens. People think better and better and suddenly the much-needed idea pops up, the issue is resolved and the meeting ends – often early.

Equality of this sort increases the intelligence of groups.

7 Give permission to tell the truth

I first learned about running meetings in a Thinking Environment from Christopher Spence. Christopher is chief executive of the National Centre for Volunteering. In his meetings he sets a standard as chair that virtually any organization or company right now could emulate. His meeting structure is simple. The amazing thing about it is that people who attend his meetings cannot tell you exactly what he does as chair that is so effective. His meetings just happened to be 'the best' they've ever been to.

Christopher's meeting structure turns ordinary meetings on their head because it establishes the Thinking Environment components throughout. From the very first moment the structure ensures a high ratio of appreciation, equality, a certain amount of ease, a culture of listening with respect, permission to feel and the sharing of truthful information.

In fact, sharing the truth has always been crucial to the success of his meetings. After the opening positive round he goes round the group again systematically to get everyone's ideas. He reminds them that he wants to know what they really think, what the truth about the situation is as they see it. He does not want them to abdicate or capitulate or fabricate.

On one such occasion the group was discussing a difficulty. In her turn one woman said, 'Can we be negative yet?'

Christopher said, 'You can say anything you think about this topic. Until the closing round, it can be as negative as it needs to be.'

'Oh, I don't have anything negative I want to say, I just wanted to know that I could,' she said.

Another person said, 'This way of having meetings really is different. It is not the way I am used to. In my other jobs the senior management team sat in front and all the rest of us lined the edge of the room and never spoke. That always concerned me because I knew that everyone had a lot to say – things that needed saying.'

The most common objection people raise to running meetings this way is that it will take too long and the work won't get done. Christopher is reassuring about this in his book *On Watch* (Cassell, 1997):

> Running a meeting as a Thinking Environment will increase the chances of people leaving the meeting with a sense of achievement, and well-connected to one another. People will anticipate the next meeting with enthusiasm rather than dread. The work will get done *and* more efficiently when time is taken to hear from each person.

Christopher is good at relating one-to-one with people and for years I attributed the innovative thinking in his meetings to his interpersonal skills. They no doubt are significant. But as the years have gone on, I have seen how central the meeting *structure* is to his meetings' success.

8 Allow people's feelings

Pain can come out of nowhere. I was working in a corporation with a senior team to develop it into a Thinking Environment. The team meeting of ten executives, all male, began just after lunch. But during lunch the whispers began. Alan, a senior colleague, had just an hour before died while delivering a speech to one of the company divisions. One moment he had been speaking and pointing to details on his slides. The next moment he was dead. The men on the executive team heard about Alan's death during their lunch.

The chair of the team suspected, rightly, that if any thinking at all was to be done at that meeting, he would have to mention Alan's death. It would be on everyone's mind. Usually this sort of thing would have been ignored and regarded as inappropriate for a business meeting. But he followed the Thinking Environment principle for sharing feelings when they block thinking.

He began by saying, 'All of us are aware I am sure that Alan Hammond died a few hours ago while delivering a talk in Howard Hall. I would like to suggest that we each take a turn to say something about what Alan meant to us and how we are feeling about the news of his death.'

No one resisted. Each man spoke. They spoke of their affection for Alan. One man said, 'The thing I feel most is remorse. I never actually told Alan how much respect and admiration I had for him. I thought it, but I never said it. I now wish I had.'

After each person had had a turn, somehow the chair sensed that that had not been sufficient, that there was more that needed saying. So he went around again.

'I want to re-prioritize things, take better care of myself, do now more of what is important,' said one man.

'I can't imagine what Betty [Alan's wife] must be going through right this minute,' said another.

The chair went around a third time. This time a few of them passed, saying they had nothing more they needed to say. Others spoke again. One man, unembarrassed by his tears, said, 'Alan and I started at this company together, twenty-two years ago. I cannot imagine work here without him.'

Then the film over the group, the collective despondency, had begun to lift just enough, and the chair decided to begin the business agenda. The meeting was subdued but productive. The agenda was finished efficiently and the team members appreciated each other at the end.

The chair told me that he was certain that if he had ignored Alan's death and ploughed on with the meeting, no clear or useful ideas would have come forth and the time would have been wasted. Taking time to hear from everyone, taking time to face reality, had saved time.

9 End with a positive turn

It is similarly important to end the meeting, after all the business is done and all the negative things have been said, with a final *positive* round. Appreciate both the meeting and each other.

a) *First reflect positively on the meeting.*

After the business is completed and negative issues have been examined, ask a question like: 'What do you think went well in the meeting?' Regardless of how difficult the meeting was and regardless of how low the spirits of the group might be at the close of business, to articulate what was good about the meeting, truthfully, will brighten the group, remind each person of what is true and good between them, and re-ignite the group's energy. Most important, it will help each person think more clearly until the next meeting.

Be sure not to permit negative reflections at this point. Ending this way prevents the phenomenon of 'negative group affect', the pulling-down of everyone. It is amazing to watch the positive change that inevitably comes over the group when the meeting ends with a truthful, affirming round.

b) *Then appreciate each other.*

Follow the first question with this one: 'What is one quality that you respect in the person sitting on your right?' Give everyone a turn to say that to the person next to them. Insist that the recipient listen without interrupting the speaker and then merely say, without rebuttal or caveat, 'Thank you.'

Most colleagues go through months and months, some even years, some their whole career, not giving or hearing recognition and appreciation from their peers. What they do not realize is that *people's thinking improves* noticeably when they are *in the presence of concrete appreciation.*

Pulling this off will take more aplomb from you than will the other meeting components. But it will be worth all the apparent risk. The intelligence of individuals and groups opens in this particular light.

Resistance

There is nothing complicated in the structure of these meetings. The proposed simple changes without embellishment create a profound difference. Meetings run along the lines described have saved millions of lives, valuable talent and hundreds of millions of pounds. But for a combination of reasons, leaders may at first resist changing. They need encouragement, and training, to do it.

Many people chairing meetings are afraid that what is unusual about this Thinking Environment structure will cause discomfort, criticism or even rebellion in the group. Throughout graduate school and within the 'tough-is-best' culture that can characterize our organizational life, people have been trained to regard the collaborative, respectful, un-urgent conditions of a TE as soft, 'touchy/feely' and weak. Some people are afraid that if they listen incisively, ask questions respectfully, give everyone a turn, allow space for thinking and balance criticism with commendation, they will be regarded as wimps.

The Thinking Environment culture also *does not produce an adrenaline rush* from such things as attack, competition between people and interruption. Some people are addicted to adrenaline. Without this false sense of being alive, they can feel lethargic and under-stimulated. For some people listening incisively to another person is actually physically uncomfortable because their heart is beating so rapidly from chronic anxiety.

Therefore, even the indisputable results of a Thinking Environment (in the quality of the ideas produced, in the business results from those ideas and in the added inclusiveness, buy-in and team enthusiasm that follow a Thinking Environment meeting) can still be outweighed for some people by the discomfort they can feel when required to behave in this new, Thinking Environment way. One man said, 'This Thinking Environment model works. I see its value. I admit we probably should be using it most of the time. But I don't like it. I prefer combat.' So they just don't do it. With strong, well-trained leadership and team practice, however, this 'tough-guy' anxiety and addiction to adrenaline in team members subsides and is replaced with positive enjoyment both of the Thinking Environment process and its obvious and valuable results.

It brings, as Jim Maclean, the leader of a senior team at HM Customs and Excise said, real and lasting changes in the way your senior management team operates.

Brainstorming in a Thinking Environment

Brainstorming has become the staple food of groups searching for ideas. It is a useful technique because it prevents the thinking inhibitor of judgement. But it is even more effective if you apply to it the standards of a Thinking Environment. Next time someone suggests you brainstorm something, suggest that everyone get a turn in sequence first to put forward an idea. Then open it to random contributions, but do not allow interruption. Then intermittently do another systematic round to hear from everyone. And at least once divide into pairs and give the pair a total of, say, ten minutes to go back and forth between themselves, producing one idea per person.

The problem with traditional brainstorming is that it gets ideas mostly from the quickest few people in the group and it gets only the easily accessible ideas from them. The often better ideas that are down a little bit further need a chance to be mined too. The Thinking Environment structure gets the best from everyone.

Virtual Meetings

Chairing my first transatlantic video meeting I noticed one good thing among all the rather stilted features of that set-up: the technology prevented interruption. That was a surprising benefit to find in the sea of cables and mice and monitors. In fact, a two-second delay in voice transmission meant that you actually had to wait a teeny bit past the point when the person talking had finished – rudiments of a Thinking Environment.

Virtual meetings, whether you love them or loathe them, will only proliferate. Simultaneously, the 'real' human features of a Thinking Environment will become more and more important as an antidote to our being only images on a screen rather than flesh across a table. In particular, creative ways of showing 'cyber attention' for people will be crucial in order for people to do their best thinking 'together' in this way.

Caroline Allen of the No-Nonsense Team of Consultants said in a speech she made at a renowned management college in Britain:

> In the next century organizations will become increasingly virtual: places in cyberspace with fluid workforces; where time means everything and space means nothing, where structures cannot be defined on graph paper.
>
> In this world organizations will be the *relationships* between the players: the employees, the customers, the suppliers and the varied communities in which the networked organization operates. *The relationships will be all that actually exist.*
>
> Discovering what individuals can offer will no longer be possible by standing over their backs with a stop watch. As physical tasks become more and more the domain of the robot, people's contribution will be the result of what they think, not what they do. Creating a Thinking Environment for each other then becomes ever more essential.
>
> The dynamics of the relationship between two thinking partners *are* the building blocks of tomorrow's organizations.

Pauline Sandell of London and Phoenix is now experimenting with Thinking Circles through the Internet. How to keep the 'rounded, fluid' quality of in-person listening while using a keyboard and not-in-real-time attention is the first challenge.

I predict that new Thinking Environment technology will be a major product development within the next five years. It seems that once people experience a Thinking Environment, they want it all the time; and they will find real and virtual ways to get it.

The Ease of It

Running a meeting as a Thinking Environment doesn't have to be hard. If a team leader or meeting chair has courage, finesse and even a mildly adventurous spirit, they can run a meeting in this way and get good reviews and good outcomes.

One of the best moments in meetings like this is the sudden new flash of an idea across someone's face in the middle of their own sentence. *Knowing* they would not be interrupted, they have relaxed somewhere, they have loaded up their hearts with a bit more than usual self-esteem and they speak.

As they speak, they have time to hear themselves. *They think because they speak.* Often it is in that same moment, when the adrenaline-infused, self-promoting listener, desperate to interrupt, suddenly deflates with a thud. Their idea that seemed like a Nobel prize grabber only seconds before doesn't even have to be said. Because there was no interruption, something different and truly good was conceived. Whether people like it or not, they learn humility in a Thinking Environment.

Basically this format creates a meeting worth a billion pounds – sometimes literally, and always spiritually. The important thing about the structure is that it is real and uncomplicated. Good ideas are incipient in everyone's brain, waiting to be formed and spoken. You don't have to do anything fancy in a meeting to produce those ideas. You just have to create these conditions and the ideas will emerge. Don't, however, let the simplicity fool you. It can unleash the power of your whole organization. This is because people hear ideas of a calibre they don't often hear and from people who don't otherwise speak. One manager said of a member of her team, 'I heard more ideas from Jason in this meeting than I have in the three whole years he has been here. I didn't know he could think like that. Maybe we never gave him a chance.'

Exactly.

CHAPTER 16

Timed Talk

Synergy takes place
best in structure.

'I went into my boss's office today,' said Yvonne. 'She asked me to sit down. Then she began talking. I did not interrupt her. That was OK for a while, but she suddenly started gathering speed and did not draw breath from one sentence to the next. Gradually what she said was a problem to be solved became a diatribe against me and then escalated into real nutso stuff. She was even screaming at me at one point.

'I'd guess that little pathological power dump lasted a good ten minutes. I was like a building site when she'd finished. I could not think. I wanted to scream back, but I didn't dare. It was awful. So I went cold and said I would think about what she had said and I left. Obviously listening without interruption was not so great for me that time. What should I have done instead? Help!'

So I told her about Timed Talk. Basically this is a way to have a fight in a Thinking Environment – or rather it is a way to *not* have a fight. It is a way to keep thinking when the tension is fierce, disagreement is solid and all you want is to win. It is also perfect for creative cross-fire. It is a way to develop new ideas with someone, going back and forth, achieving synergy and bringing ideas to maturity in record time.

This structure is committed essentially to one thing: preventing interruption when feelings are inflamed. This structure recognizes that interruption does violence to the formation of ideas.

For instance, you begin speaking to someone and something you say upsets her. She cuts you off before you finish your thought. That upsets *you* and your adrenaline kicks in. She is up and running about what you have just said (never mind that she doesn't actually *know* what you just said because she did not let you finish). You can't concentrate because you are smarting from her interruption. You are looking madly for a micro-space in which to interrupt her, and you do.

She boils. She hears an infinitesimal bit of your string of words and then clobbers all of it by interrupting you. This really upsets you. You sweat. Your diaphragm throbs. And you yell back, 'Well, then, suck an egg!' and you walk off. Or perhaps you don't say, 'Suck an egg!', but you definitely walk off. As you walk away, you realize with a cool clunk that you will have to start all over with her some time in the next few hours or days because your original issue has not been remotely resolved. It is lying bludgeoned to bits somewhere between you.

That failure was a product not of the divergent opinions between you on the subject, but of the interruptions. Try to imagine a discussion taking place lucidly between hits in the face, blows on the head and arms in a full Nelson. Verbal interruption has a similar effect on thinking and discussion. It assaults and as with any fight it triples the time needed to reach a resolution. First there is the fight, which did not work. Then there is the apology, which sometimes takes ages. Then there is the attempt to have the discussion again. And if interruption prevails a second time, the thing becomes a dinosaur before you work it out. At the very least, that is inefficient. At worst it creates cold wars. Regardless, it is not thinking. In such a situation Timed Talk can help.

How Timed Talk Works

You agree that you are about to have this difficult discussion. Beware of the denial: '*You* may be fighting, but I'm not.' That is a sure indication that the fight has just begun.

Set a timer for three minutes. If this seems too organized for words, think of the timer as the neutral boundary keeper, the dispassionate referee.

One of you goes first. Be generous. She talks for three minutes. You do not say a single word. I'd even be cautious about 'uh huh' under these conditions. If you can, you keep your eyes on her eyes and a facial expression of respect and encouragement. But if you can't manage that, the bottom line is you have to stay in the room, within hearing range. And you cannot interrupt her. Or turn on the TV. Or knit.

Finally, after centuries, the timer goes off. She has to stop even mid-word. It is your turn to say whatever you want (though remember there *is* life after this thing and you don't want to say anything you will regret later. Don't be nasty. Think about your future). Remember that you will not be interrupted for a whole three minutes. Of course, your three-minute turn whizzes by whereas hers crept. Don't check the timer – it is not broken. This is what Einstein meant by relativity.

The timer chimes and it is her turn again. And she talks for three minutes while you listen – again. For ages.

Then it is your turn once more, then hers, and so on until you resolve the issue.

What do you do if you run out of things to say but your three minutes are not up? Do not be generous this time. You will resent it. Just keep track of your unused time and 'save' it. You may want to add it to your next turn.

And what do you do if what you need in *your* turn is feedback or information from your partner? Ask for it. Listen to it, and the second she has said all you want to hear, stop her. This is *your* turn and you, for the rest of the three minutes, are god.

For several turns the two of you might as well be speaking in tongues for as much as you will really take in of each other's point. But that is all right. Anger is dissipating in these turns and, most important, because there is equality and no interruption, no irrelevant tension is being created.

Eventually you begin to hear each other. You might not acknowledge this at first. Pride and competition have a grip on your generosity. But in spite of yourself you begin to notice the occasional intelligent point being made by the other person and she even seems to hear something worthwhile in what you have said. You know you are at this point when you no longer are desperate to have your turn and have stopped being sure the timer is rigged in her favour. Life seems balanced all of a sudden. Nothing mysterious has happened here. It is simply that you have both begun to think instead of react. The lack of interruption has established a structure of respect and soon that structure produces real respect between you. Respect creates intellectual safety, the best environment for thinking.

I have seen people take a full hour of three-minute turns in particularly difficult discussions. That may seem like a long time, but go back and remember how long a few of your fights lasted. Some last twenty years. Sometimes, however, because of the structure of no interruption, a Timed Talk takes a *very* short time and difficult things become easy quickly.

Timed Talk at a Glance

Do these things without fail:

- Set a timer for three minutes.
- Take turns talking, three minutes each. Take as many turns as necessary to resolve the issue.
- Do not interrupt each other or take over each other's turn, no matter what.
- If you don't need all of the time in one turn, save it for your next turn.
- Stop talking the instant the timer goes off.

Do these things if you can:

- Keep eye contact with the other person when they are speaking.
- Focus on finding a good idea, not on winning.
- Remember how intelligent you both are.
- Be fascinated by the other person's mind at work.
- Remember that there is an idea neither of you has yet thought of that will resolve the problem better than you can imagine.
- Smile once in a while (appropriately).
- Avoid saying things you will regret.
- Breathe out.
- If time runs out before you find a mutually good idea, schedule a time soon to continue.

Creative Cross-fire and Synergy

The Timed Talk process is not just for fights. It also fuels creativity. It progresses ideas. If you and a colleague or friend are in the planning stages of a new project or are searching for new ideas about something or just want to explore a topic, timed uninterrupted turns can be a scintillating, successful way of doing it.

Synergy of ideas is delicious. It is best achieved if you have the freedom of knowing you won't be interrupted, while also having a short, mutually agreed amount of time to think out loud. You can cross-fertilize without aborting the other person's turn. Ideas reach maturity fast this way. The only tricky part is getting your colleague or friend to agree to use the structure in the first place. But be creative. Even if you cannot use a timer, find a way to give each other approximately equal turns.

Some people say they don't like structure of any kind. They think structure kills spontaneity. But this structure actually feeds it. Some people think that free-for-all shoot-outs are more productive, but those ravage green ideas. Actually, non-structures are structures too. The only difference is that they don't work. Equal turns do.

CHAPTER 17

Presenting This Way

**Providing the presenter
with a Thinking Environment
is the key job of the audience.**

I ache when I observe presentations. I know that the presenting team has spent sometimes months doing the research, making the slides and overheads, perfecting the graphics and encouraging each other not to be scared to death.

The brave lead speaker begins. If they are lucky they get perhaps five, six sentences out and perhaps one good slide up on the screen before polish gives way to survival. Even that much is real luck, because hovering between the presenter's every word and the mouths of the gathered scrutinizers is interruption, coiled and poised to strike.

The onlookers are there to cast judgement. They have been taught that *they* must look good. And that means piping up with an objection, a critical question, an attack on the data or the validity of the conclusion as soon as humanly possible. Once in a while, of course, to wait very long to ask a crucial clarifiying question or to correct the data is to render the presentation pointless, but that is actually rare. Far too much of the time the individuals in the audience are salivating for attack, often just to dazzle their colleagues.

As with ordinary meetings presentations convene for the ostensible purpose of igniting ideas and pointing the way forwards. The personal image agenda of the observers, however, thwarts that. It also weakens and lengthens the presentations themselves – as well as the confidence of the presenters.

Presentations should be occasions for doubled enthusiasm, for a fresh picture of what the project can achieve. Even if the presentation has huge flaws, these can be welcomed rather than dreaded if they are addressed in a Thinking Environment. But all too often during presentations the presenters experience a slow seepage of self-esteem.

Not impressed with these results, I recommend a Thinking Environment structure for presentations. It goes something like this:

1 The chair welcomes the presenting team and mentions its successes so far.

2 The presenters make *the entire presentation* before there is any interruption or attack. (If you are confused about something, so confused you truly cannot listen to the next sentence, ask for clarification, but only if you are sure the question is not going to be answered in the next sentence or two.)

3 After the presentation is complete, the chair asks first for comments on what was useful from the presentation, demonstrating this by being first to speak.

4 Then the chair encourages questions and discussion, but always *without interruption.*

5 At the end of the meeting, regardless of how much legitimate criticism there has been of the presentation, the chair goes around the group to get honest answers to this question: What do you think has been good in this presentation, and what in particular do you respect in the presenting team?

By definition nothing about a Thinking Environment structure can be rigid. So as chair of presentation meetings you will have to adapt this format to the demand of the moment. But hang on to the principles behind this. If you do, presentations can become things people look forward to. They may go away from the meeting feeling smarter rather than crushed. That is worth your taking the lead on how it will be run.

As always, you can make an enormous difference just by setting up a Thinking Environment wherever you are.

CHAPTER 18

Supervising This Way

Management supervision
is an opportunity
to bring people back to themselves.

'She is so charismatic and so good with words that, when she was my boss, I hardly ever said anything.'

Believe it or not, this is a management supervision being described. If it had been a movie or holy communion, fine. Not much talking is required from those recipients. But in supervision the point is for the recipient to think well. That means talking and being listened to. Leave your charisma and long-winded wisdom for later. What is required is your attention. The recipient does the talking. You, their manager, for a long time, do the listening.

Begin with the good things. Consider these questions:

- What do you think you have accomplished in this period?
- What has gone particularly well?
- What are you proud of?
- What have you discovered about yourself?
- What is the key thing that you want to improve?
- What might you be assuming that could stop you?
- If you assumed something more freeing, what would your first step be?
- What sort of support do you need from me in order to do it?
- What do you think your goals and targets for this next period should be?

- And what will your performance indicators be?
- What other issues do you want to raise with me?
- If it were entirely up to you, what would you like to see improve in our working relationship?

Listen to their answers, fully. Do not even think about interrupting. Then respond. Be honest with your assessment: generous with your appreciation and focused with your criticism. People need a context of genuine praise in which to make changes. They need succinct proposals for change in order to make progress.

People shine not in the glow of your charisma. They shine in the light of your attention for them. It is from that that they can see their own brilliance. They shine when you remind them that they matter.

Supervision is an opportunity to bring someone home to their own mind, to show them how good they can be, to demonstrate how problems can be solved and dignity gained.

CHAPTER 19

Change in a Thinking Environment

Change at this pace
absolutely requires
that people think for themselves.

Change is no longer the hot issue in organizations. It is endemic. It is now the *pace* of change that kills.

'It used to be like standing on the beach when waves come in, belly-flopping on top of each other,' said Duncan, 'but now it is like being sucked down by a tidal wave. You can hardly stand upright before the next one hits.'

The only real tool to handle it is thinking – thinking on your feet so that you don't fall to your knees. In managing change, you have to listen better than ever. You have to understand that change means loss and loss requires grieving. I am not saying you have to be people's death therapists. Please don't be. But just as you would, I hope, if a member of your team experienced a personal bereavement, you must ask how they are *and listen.*

My colleague Vanessa, president of Going Well, asked a senior civil servant how his managers were coping with the breakers of change that crash hourly on to the civil service. 'I have no idea,' he said. 'I don't ask them.'

'Why?' she asked.

'They might tell me.' Vanessa listened, curious. 'We couldn't have that,' he concluded.

What he was really saying was that *he* couldn't handle that. His qualification for leadership had not included the mastery of a Thinking Environment. It should have. His staff was suffering; and their work showed it. Absenteeism was proliferating; work output was down. Leaders pay a steep price for avoiding the truth of people's experience.

So in the face of change add to any other intelligent strategies this one:

1 Give correct information about the upcoming changes as soon as you possibly can and as succinctly.

2 Give everyone a turn, in groups or in private, to say how they really feel about the changes.

3 Ask them what ideas they have for adapting. Find out what they might be assuming that could stop them from making a good transition, even if the changes mean their redundancy.

4 Listen, listen, listen.

5 Appreciate their good work.

The fifth point is particularly important. 'It wouldn't have been so bad,' a project leader said, 'if they had at least praised our project before they shut it down. We had worked on it for two years. But they said nothing. Our interest in the next project was tiny as a result.'

Listening, appreciating, asking, giving timely information, giving everyone a turn – these things that work so well and matter so much are not complicated to do. They may require your discomfort for a little while as you get used to them. But with practice your discomfort will pass. Change won't.

CHAPTER 20

Peer Mentoring

Peer mentoring
is of highest quality when listening
and Incisive Questions are its core.

Peer mentoring and a Thinking Environment were made for each other. I heartily support the concept of people at work becoming mentors for each other. That relationship is one of equals. It is supportive of each person's growth and excellence. It is on tap. And it is free. I have found that when people advance their skills with each other by giving attention in the ways I have described, and by understanding the power and construction of Incisive Questions, the value of their time together as mentors increases hugely.

Mentoring each other fails to be effective when

- the mentor does not listen long or well enough;
- the mentor considers that their primary purpose is to tell the mentored what to do.

Mentoring works best if it is interpreted as a mutually supportive time to think. Advice or direction or ideas from the mentor are not always inappropriate, but they should come as a very last resort, after the person has had an uninterrupted turn to speak freely, remove their own limiting assumptions and find their own ideas.

Some peer mentors find the formal Thinking Session (Chapters 26–31) a helpful format. But peer mentoring can make use of even one of the Thinking Environment principles and skills to very good effect.

Just not to be interrupted, for example, until you have said everything, to be paid high-quality attention by your mentor, means that more of your mind is available and better ideas and greater energy can emerge. People are reporting very good results from applying this theory and practice to the already-superb idea of people at work mentoring each other.

CHAPTER 21

Leading This Way

**Today's leader must prize the minds
of people above all else.**

The first job of a leader is to create a Thinking Environment, from top to bottom. This means listening long and with ease, and asking Incisive Questions. In particular, leaders of thinking organizations should take the following words to heart:

Prize the quality of your attention
- Listen as if your leadership life depended on it. It does.
- When you make mistakes, listen to the effects of them. Apologize. Correct them.
- Appreciate five times more than you criticize.
- Stop competing with your colleagues. Encourage their excellence. Trust that your own will be evident.
- Set up a Thinking Partnership with a colleague. Meet three times a week for fifteen-minute turns each.
- Run every meeting and presentation as a Thinking Environment (see Chapters 15 and 17).

Become known for your Incisive Questions
Ask these questions often of your team or staff:
1 What do you really think?
2 If you were in my position, what would you do with this company that I am not doing?

3 What do we as an organization assume that probably limits everything we do? If we were to assume something more freeing, what would change?

4 At the end of your career in this organization, what do you want to say you have achieved here when you look back?

5 What needs improvement in this organization that I haven't noticed? If you had to take the lead suddenly, what would you do about it?

6 What are we not facing that is in front of our face?

7 How would your work have to change for it to be exactly right for you?

8 If you were not holding back, what would you be doing?

9 What do we already know now that we are going to find out in a year?

Ask these questions often of yourself:

1 What do I assume about myself most of the time that is limiting my leadership? If I were to assume something more liberating, what would change?

2 If I weren't afraid, what would I be risking?

3 If I already knew that I am good and admired, how would I champion others today?

4 If I were to be my *real* self in my leadership, what would I do differently?

5 Whom among the people most junior to me can I invite to think with me today?

6 What can I do today to create more of a Thinking Environment in the organization?

7 What would I have to do to set up dependable thinking time for myself every day?

Leaders create. A creator's best tool is a Thinking Environment. Without it, leaders fall back into ticking the list. And when mediocrity, or even demise, sets into the bones of their organization, they find, if they can bear to look back, that the ten components of a Thinking Environment languished too long, visitors on the periphery. Embrace them: they are the bedrock of leadership that lasts.

CHAPTER 22

Executive Coaching

The brilliant executive coach
is the one who brings out
the brilliance of the client.

Support for leaders and executives is crucial. The higher people fly in an organization, the less contact they have with the work on the ground; thus the more insular their thinking can become and the more detached they can become from the heart of the people they serve. An objective 'outsider' who can feel an accurate pulse of the whole organization and give a global business or organizational overview, and who can be at least a good sounding board, helps a leader decisively. Coaching is proliferating because it is desperately needed.

But as it is usually done, it is limited. It can lack the integrity, precision and non-infantilizing infrastructure of a Thinking Environment. Coaching can, however, transmute into something truly superb if coaches can become expert at two processes.

One is giving stunning, nearly serene *attention* to your client for much, much longer than you have been accustomed to do. This will mean reinterpreting your job as coach. You are not primarily a Vesuvius of analysis and advice any more. You are to be a Thinking Environment for your client. That will mean listening so well that your client is directed back to their own thinking over and over. Even if they expect your advice, you will be most effective if you keep them doing their own best thinking first. After that has happened thoroughly, you can tell them what you think. They will hear you better then anyway. And if you are very good at being a Thinking Partner to them, you may not, except for any information they may lack, have to tell them very much.

The second process at which you will need to become expert is asking *Incisive Questions*. When executive coaches have trained in this they have invariably reported great success, sometimes even excitement, after they have made use of Incisive Questions with their clients.

One acclaimed executive coach I know, Tina Breene, said in an interview recently:

> The danger with coaching lies in the perceived need for the coach to appear brilliant, to be seen to have all the answers. When coaches are focused on looking wonderfully clever, they do not listen long enough. They summarize and interpret and direct far too early in the session.
>
> Coaches need to realize that the brilliant person is the client. The coach's job is to help the client discover that. The real expert on the organization is not the coach, however informed and experienced they may be. The real expert is the person who is running the organization.

A Thinking Environment gives the client space to find out what they already know and to think of new ideas themselves, ideas that will work.

Giving insight and direction to the client is not incompatible with a Thinking Environment coaching session. Sometimes it is exactly what is needed. But let that kind of directive intervention come later, after everything else has failed.

Ironically, by bringing out the brilliance in the client, you as coach will be seen as the brilliant one.

CHAPTER 23

Reciprocity:
The Individual and the Organization

An organization is a 'person' too.

An organization consists of individuals and is itself an individual. A thinking organization is two rivers flowing through each other. On the one hand, individuals in the organization are being treated to a Thinking Environment. At the same time they are providing the organization with a Thinking Environment as if it too were a human being.

The individual, for example, listens to the organization to hear what it is experiencing, what is really happening in it, what its fears are, where it is heading, what it needs. The individual enters the organization each day with ease and avoids inflicting urgency or tension on it. The individual, for instance, does not create emergencies in order to feel personally alive or important.

Individuals give a thinking organization as much as they get from it. They make sure that the organization has its turn to speak, to be represented in discussion alongside the talk of individuals about their work. Individuals appreciate a thinking organization publicly five times more than they criticize it. They give the organization accurate, full information; they do not lie to it or use it for duplicitous ends. Individuals encourage the organization to be all it can be; they do not compete with it by trying to star at the organization's expense. Individuals see to it that the physical place of the organization is respected, is clean, is furnished and looked after in such a way that it knows it matters.

Individuals keep on the look-out for assumptions the organization is making about itself or the world that are limiting what it can do and how well it can do it. Individuals pose this question often: 'What might we as an organization or a team be assuming that could be limiting our thinking here; and if we were to assume something more freeing, what new ideas would we have?'

Individuals insist on diversity in the organization, not settling for all male, middle-aged, middle-class, heterosexual, able-bodied people in leadership. They make sure rampant homogeneity is challenged and changed.

Individuals notice when something has touched the nerve centre of the organization and made it sad or depressed or angry. They hold appropriate events for the whole organization to gather and acknowledge the impact it has experienced. In that way feelings can be sorted out and clear thinking can resume.

In a thinking organization these ten components flow continuously through the individuals and the organization. Both thrive only if the Thinking Environment is reciprocal between them. This kind of reciprocity should be part of our definition of equality. Each of us matters, but what we create matters too, and how we treat our creation determines how it will treat us. We depend on each other. We are both.

II. A Turn of Your Own: The Thinking Partnership

CHAPTER 24

The Thinking Session: Introduction

A Thinking Partnership
is a personal and
professional imperative.

A Thinking Environment belongs in two settings: in public, which we have explored, and in private.

In public there is a limit to the amount of safety available to people to think for themselves. People in organizations, for example, are committed to sticking to work-related issues. They also are sometimes afraid of reprisal should they reveal subjective things about themselves.

In private, one to one with a colleague or friend, a Thinking Environment can be established with safety and no risk. In a Thinking Partnership like this, you can trust the pledge of confidentiality. You can speak freely. You can search for and remove bedrock assumptions about yourself and the world. Lasting change occurs here.

Until life rewards people for thinking for themselves, we will have to create special circumstances in which to do it. Thinking Sessions are such havens. Many people establish this liberating structure on a weekly basis and find that its fruits extend past the joy of personal development back into the wider world. Personal change does, it seems, form the foundation for change in society.

A Thinking Session is an inviolable time in your day when you and a friend or colleague have equal amounts of time to think *for yourself* about a topic of your choice. You agree to give each other attention, not to interrupt each other, not to judge, not to take over, nor during the session to give each other ideas. You also agree to ask Incisive Questions at the appropriate time in order to remove the stubborn blocks of limiting assumptions. Throughout you agree to respect each other for the very act of thinking for yourself.

The six-part Thinking Session is a formal discipline, but it is not a contrivance. It is a reconstruction of a natural process that we observed over many years. It can seem 'artificial' because in its natural form in everyday life it rarely has a chance to complete itself before someone ramrods it with interruption and advice. We hardly ever see it in full.

The Six-part Thinking Session: Origins

It started in an eighteenth-century restaurant in Middleburg, Virginia, about twelve years ago. I was having lunch with my new friend Penny. We were having what I thought was a perfectly ordinary conversation about her life.

She was telling me that she wanted to find more time to be with her family but not quit her job. I was listening along and asking the occasional casual question, between bites and glances at the log fire.

Then suddenly, in a much-too-loud voice, she said, 'Stop!'

I looked at her and put down my fork.

'Right there! That is it. That is what I want to understand.'

'What?' I asked her, noticing the women in pearls and wool jackets frowning at us.

'What were you thinking inside your own head,' she said, 'just before you asked me that question?' Her voice grew louder. 'The very second before. What was it?'

'Jeeze, I don't know, Penny. I can't even remember what I asked you,' I said in a determined whisper, shooting an apologetic smile at the pearls.

Penny pulled the huge linen napkin out from her lap and began to fold it. I thought she might be going to leave.

She said, 'I said I want to work less, earn more and spend more time with the family. Then I said that Mark would be angry if I upset my boss. Then I said that I would not know how to handle Mark's anger. And you said, "If you knew that *you can handle anything* Mark might do or say, what change would you propose to your boss?" And bingo I had an idea of how I could restructure my job. Just like that, out of nowhere. And it happened right after you asked that question.'

'Well, good,' I said, taking a sip of water. 'I'm glad.'

'No,' Penny said. 'I don't want you to be glad. What I want is to know what *caused* you to think of that question? I figure something must have been going on in your head that made you think of it. So what was it?'

'I have no idea,' I said.

She put her napkin back in her lap. 'Well, try,' she said. I did. It took me seven years.

The Thinking Session is what eventually emerged from that exploration. It is a formal, disciplined prototype of a Thinking Environment. It consists of six parts, beginning with open-ended time to think. It progresses from one part to the next logically and easily, removing limiting assumptions that block a person's thinking.

Sometimes Part 1 is enough. But sometimes, even after all the listening you can offer, the Thinker still wants more from the session. It is at this juncture (or long before it most of the time) that, in ordinary conversation, the listener kicks in with *their* ideas and tells the Thinker what to think. But my colleagues and I wondered whether there still might be ideas inside the Thinker's head that we had just not yet accessed. We wondered whether those ideas might be blocked by something that the highest-calibre attention of Part 1 had not budged.

The search for and removing of blocks became a passion. We refused to believe that running out of ideas and into blocks indicated that a person's mind had done all it could do on its own. Perhaps, instead, there was a systematic way to remove those blocks. And, if so, what other brilliant ideas *of the Thinker's own* might lie on the other side? I was absorbed in that one question for years.

What, we wondered, might the blocks be? How could we find them? And how could we remove them?

The six-part structure of the Thinking Session eventually emerged out of the search for those answers. The session is the result of noticing and piecing together the structure that was naturally there in good thinking.

The Six Parts

Those six parts, now so clear, flexible and dependable, were for years a murky mass. At least, they were to me – until a few years ago when I was in Texas for my seminar there. My sister Merl and her husband Lovell had organized the event. I was working on my notes for the course.

I had been trying for about a year to write an essay on how to do a Thinking Session so that the participants might make it work for themselves. But the material I had written didn't seem to teach people very well.

Lovell looked up from reading the newspaper and asked to see my page of notes. I gave it to him, pleased he was interested. While he read my sheets, I thumbed through *Southwest Cattle,* not engrossed, looking out of the corner of my eye at Lovell, curious about the marks he was making.

'Oh,' he said, 'I see. There are six parts to this thing.'

'There are?' I asked. My heart leapt at the thought that there might be some discernible order to this process that people seemed to consider magic.

'Sure,' he said, as if he had just pointed out that birds fly. 'Right here. There are six parts. First you listen to the person in a random sort of way. Right?'

'Random?' I think I sounded offended.

'Well, OK, open. Not much intervention is what I mean.'

'Right.' I smiled.

'Then you determine their goal for the session, what they want out of it after they have talked enough.'

'Yes,' I said.

'Then you find out their assumption, the one blocking them from getting what they want from the session now.'

I nodded, fascinated. Why hadn't I seen this structure?

'Then you ask the – what do you call it? – explicit question.'

'Incisive,' I said.

'Exactly,' he said. 'Then you tell them to write that down. Then they appreciate each other. Six. There it is.'

He handed me back the paper. I guess it is true that there is nearly always order in disorder. Six parts it was. Bliss.

Some moments in life are like that. Change doesn't always have to be hard or take a long time. (It probably helps, though, to know someone like Lovell.)

In skilled hands, the Thinking Session moves from the first thoughts of the Thinker, right through the process of asking Incisive Questions (the kind of question Penny was so adamant about) in order to remove blocks called limiting assumptions, and out to fresh new ideas of the Thinker's own. It is usually elegant. It is always liberating. But it takes some instruction.

In this section of the book I offer a sample Thinking Session and discuss in detail the theory and practice behind it. I hope that you will use this part of the book as an ongoing guide and as a source of encouragement to set up your own Thinking Partnership with someone and to treat yourselves, at least once a week, to the powerful effects of a Thinking Session.

CHAPTER 25

Kyle's Session

Dead men don't smile.

If you were on a course with me, I would demonstrate for you the detail and power of a full Thinking Session. Someone would volunteer to be the Thinker and someone would be the Thinking Partner, the one who listens and asks questions. I would 'coach' and you would observe. From that experience, and especially from your own turns as Thinker and Thinking Partner, you would see this process unfold. And with enough practice, you would soon be able to perform both roles well.

However, we exist for each other only in this book at the moment, and so it will have to be on these pages that I show you how a Thinking Session works. I offer you in this chapter a narration of Kyle's Thinking Session when Eric was his Thinking Partner. Later, at the end of the book, you will get to be with Eric as he thinks his way through to his dreams while Kyle listens. In the chapters that follow, I discuss the six-part structure in detail. But I think that instruction will mean more to you if you first read the brief summary of a Thinking Session given below and then 'see' a demonstration of a real session.

The Thinking Session at a Glance

These are the effective questions:

Part 1
What do you want to think about?
Is there anything more (you think or feel or want to say about this)?

Part 2

What do you want the session to achieve at this point?

Part 3

What are you assuming (that is stopping your achieving that goal)?
   (To find the bedrock assumption:) That's possible, but what are you
   assuming that makes *that* stop you?
What is your positive opposite of that assumption?

Part 4

If you knew that (new, freeing assumption) . . . , what ideas would you
   have towards that goal?

Part 5

Write down the Incisive Question.

Part 6

What quality do you respect in each other?

Eric and Kyle agreed to have a Thinking Session while the others on the
course observed. I sat across from Eric as his coach. My role would be to
do as little as possible.

Part 1: Saying Everything

Eric began appropriately, 'What do you want to think about?'

'Time,' Kyle said.

Eric nodded.

'I need to think about my way too busy life.'

He paused. Eric kept his eyes on Kyle but did not say anything. He
wanted to say, 'Join the club.' But he didn't.

'For the fifth year in a row I have over-scheduled myself. By the end of
this month I will hardly have time to breathe. *Again.* I keep doing this.'

Eric nodded understanding but was careful not to say what he was thinking which was, 'Yeah, I remember your complaining about this last year.' He just paid attention and moved his focus back on to Kyle as a thinker, fascinated by where Kyle might go with this issue this time.

'I have also already figured out that things usually take twice as long as I think they will. So I've started to plan for that. I am not late to everything any more. So that is good.'

Kyle looked up at Eric. Eric nodded and smiled. 'I think you must be thinking that I am a jerk,' Kyle said. 'We had this conversation a year ago.'

'No, I admire you for persisting in figuring this out. And I certainly do not think you are a jerk,' Eric said.

'Well, good. But I do. Anyway.' Kyle leaned back in his chair, stretched his legs out and sighed. 'What am I going to do about this?'

Ordinarily Eric would have given Kyle some ideas. However, this time he remained quiet, assuming that Kyle was asking the question in order to get his *own* mind to think about it. Sure enough, Kyle continued.

'The problem is that I say yes to all requests. I see this sort of loose swoop of time ahead of me and I say, "Sure, no problem." But actually, although the time is not booked, it is not necessarily available either. For example, last October Jane Spritz called from the Symphony League and asked if I would serve on the board. She said it would entail bi-monthly meetings. That sounded very do-able.

'But those six days a year turned out to be eighteen. The six were just the meeting days. There were also unpredictable hours each month of reading papers, making phone calls, doing subcommittee meetings. There also were two formal dinner parties each year. So I said yes without calculating the "unofficial time". And now I have twice as much to do in the next three weeks as I can possibly do.

'That is the problem. I see these gaping open times in my diary and forget that actually they are full – with unexpected work of all sorts.

And that does not include a single family thing. Forget the family in all of this.'

Eric had a million things to say – some just chiming in and some advice – but he stayed quiet and at ease and kept paying attention to Kyle. This felt awkward and made him self-conscious, but he could see that saying nothing was working. Kyle was clearly on a roll.

'To manage it, I either have to cut . . .' Kyle paused.

Eric was tempted to finish his sentence for him with, '. . . out the Symphony League', which he was sure from the context Kyle was going to say. But he didn't.

A second later Kyle said, 'I will either have to cut corners, which I hate, or take work home in the evenings and over the weekend – which I have been doing every week now for over a year. I also hate that. My work life already goes from 7.30 in the morning until nearly 8 in the evenings. I don't like the fact that this keeps happening.' Kyle drew breath.

Eric was doing a good job. He kept listening. He kept his eyes always on Kyle's regardless of where Kyle's eyes bounced or landed. He wanted now, though, to say, 'There are such things as time management courses, you know.' But he didn't. It was good he didn't because it would have interrupted Kyle's flow and in any case Kyle would most likely have said, 'Yeah, I know, I have had four of those. They helped me structure what I am realistic about but did not even touch this thing that makes me think there is time when there isn't.' Eric gave Kyle attention and trusted.

Kyle went on. 'Nicole said to me last night, "Daddy, do you hate your work?" That shocked me because I certainly do not hate my work. I love my work. But it made me stop. I said, "No, honey, I really enjoy my work. Why?" And she said, "Oh, nothing, you just don't smile any more."'

Kyle looked at Eric and then away. There was a long silence, long enough to make Eric wonder if he should be doing anything. But he stuck to the 'rules' and did not interrupt the quiet. He could see in the corner of Kyle's eye that he was off somewhere on his own.

As always, Kyle 'came back'. He looked straight into Eric's eyes.

There was a kind of fire, an intensity in him that made Eric uneasy. But he held his attention on Kyle and relaxed his face.

'What is Nicole learning from me, Eric – from the way I live? I would hate for her to grow up and live as I do. She is seeing something I can't see. It is a little thing, a stupid smile, but it is big too. I'm *not* happy, she's right. I do like my work, but it is killing me. Last year Alan died. Just like that. Boom. He was giving a talk in front of 200 people and wham he was on the floor in an instant and dead in the next.'

Eric knew about Alan's death and had been upset by it too, but he did not chime in with ordinary commiseration and his own memories. He said, 'I know,' and nodded, because Kyle had looked at him, raising one eyebrow as if to say, 'You understand what I mean?'

'He was my age, for Christsake,' Kyle said. Then he stopped for a second, rested his elbow on his knee and looked up at Eric, 'Dead men don't smile, Eric.'

The next moment Kyle broke away and stood up. He turned round and looked back at Eric and then walked to the window. Putting his hands on the window sill and looking down at his fingers he said, 'No one is going to do this for me.' He turned round and looked again at Eric. Eric nodded.

Kyle continued, 'I just want to ask out loud, "Is there any alternative to the endlessness of the cycles of work?"' He looked down. And then he laughed. He said, 'You may have heard (this is probably apocryphal but it gets a laugh at corporate conferences and that tells you something) about what the department store Marks and Spencer calls its Two-jacket Executive Suit: one pair of trousers and two identical jackets. Have you heard this?'

Eric shook his head.

'Well, these suits were supposedly invented at the suggestion of executives who could no longer tolerate their blistering work schedule. The executive wears one jacket and puts one on the back of his desk chair. Then he leaves to play golf or take a walk or go home early (after *only* 9 hours). The company sees his jacket on his chair and assumes he is still on the premises somewhere.'

Kyle walked back to his seat. Eric still paid attention. Kyle sighed.

'You know, this company is not going to say suddenly one day, "Oops. Sorry. Guess we've been doing this wrong. We just realized that we have overloaded you. We have been fixated on quarterly profits and we just hadn't noticed you were dropping dead. Also, you probably need a real life, family and all that. So from now on, if you don't have time to do things, just say so and we'll get it done somewhere else. You'll still be paid the same. From now it's come in at 9, leave at 5 and no weekend work." That's just not going to happen. And things like board membership requests are not going to stop. Or subcommittees or conferences or the crazed self-proliferation of everything. Are they?'

Eric didn't answer, even though he was thinking, 'Get this one figured out, buddy, and the Nobel prize is all yours.' He didn't actually think that Kyle could figure this out. He was glad at that moment that the 'rules' kept him from giving Kyle any ideas. He didn't have any.

Kyle pushed himself away from the window sill and walked back to his seat. Eric kept his eyes on Kyle's eyes and shifted his legs to get more relaxed.

'That's it,' Kyle said. 'I can't think of anything more to say.'

Then came the part of the session structure Eric found most uncomfortable – this juncture when the Thinker says he can't think of anything more to say and the Thinking Partner asks him, as if he had gone deaf, whether there is anything more he wants to say. But Eric did not show his discomfort. He said simply, 'Is there anything more you think or feel or want to say?'

Kyle chuckled, 'Good question. There is, actually. I am sick and tired of dreading my voice-mail and e-mail messages. I hate putting them off until I can face the new mudslide of demand for work that invariably saturates those things. I am now 175 e-mails behind.' There was an audible gasp across the room. 'And it has been worse than this.'

Kyle didn't say any more. He looked at the floor, then out to the flowers in the vase on the desk, then back to Eric. This time his eyes were flat. They were saying, 'I'm through.'

So Eric said, 'What else? Is there more that comes to your mind about this?'

'Yeah, one thing. I'm not the only one I know who feels this way. And I don't think it is just in this company either. I know small business people and self-employed people who feel this way too. This world is choking on its own work vomit. Something is seriously wrong in the world, Eric. More wrong than even two years ago. No one should have to live like this, loving their job but watching it eat them for breakfast.' He paused. 'That's all.'

'Anything more?' asked Eric, feeling that surely this would finally be all.

'Just that sometimes when things don't get done it turns out that they didn't need to be done. I wonder how you can figure out which ones those are ahead of time.'

Kyle looked away again. When he looked back, he was silent. And the silence quickly hardened. So Eric asked again, 'What else do you think or feel about this? Is there more?'

And with even more animation than he had had after the first asking Kyle said, 'I feel guilty thinking about doing less. I feel guilty even saying to people, "I'll get back to you," much less, "No." But I feel just as guilty about doing so much that I am a zombie and that I don't have time with Nicole. That I don't smile, apparently.' Kyle looked at Eric. 'That's all.'

'Are you sure?'

'Absolutely.'

Part 2: Recognizing What You Want to Achieve from the Rest of the Session

'OK,' Eric said, making in his own head the transition to Part 2 of the session. 'What do you want the session to achieve at this point?'

Kyle looked away. He looked back at Eric. 'What do I want the session to achieve? If it could, I don't know. That's a good question. Out of all this. Well, I would really like to figure out a way to live differently. And this time I don't want relapses.'

Eric was listening hard now to the *exact* words Kyle said: *figure out a way to live differently.* The next parts of the session would require precision.

Part 3: Finding the Limiting Assumption

'What might you be assuming that is stopping you from *figuring out a way to live differently?*' Eric asked.

Another far-away look appeared in Kyle's eyes. But Eric relaxed. The other 'trips' had been good. Kyle would 'come back'.

'Well, I guess I am assuming that my boss will question my loyalty and people like Jane will strike me off their "distinguished citizens" list if I live differently.'

'That's possible,' Eric said. 'They might. But what might you be assuming that makes that stop you from *figuring out how to live differently?*'

Kyle said, 'Could you ask me that again?'

'It's possible that those people could find you disloyal or strike you off their "distinguished citizens" list. But what are you assuming that makes that stop you from figuring out how to live differently?'

Kyle's gaze moved to the window. With space between every word as if each were just then cracking its shell he answered. 'I am assuming . . . that . . . I have no control over my life, that . . . it is . . . out of my hands. That no matter how hard I think about this . . . the lorry of my life has no driver and is on downhill ice. And I can't do a thing except hold on. Yes, I am assuming that I have no control over my life.' Kyle looked back at Eric.

I have no control over my life. Eric reasoned that Kyle might have no control over his boss and Jane, but he certainly had control over his life.

Then Eric asked Kyle what his 'positive opposite' of 'have no control' would be. Eric figured it would be 'have some control', but he knew he should get Kyle's own words in case they were different. So Eric asked, 'What is your positive opposite of "have no control over my life"?'

Kyle replied without hesitation, 'That I am the only one who *does* have control over my life.'

Eric was glad he had asked. That was subtly but powerfully different.

Part 1: Asking the Incisive Question

Eric quickly formed the Incisive Question in his head, joining Kyle's assumption and his session goal: '*If you knew that you are the only one who does have control over your life, what would you do to live differently?*'

Kyle looked at Eric and then out the window. About five seconds passed with no sound. He smiled. 'Hmm,' he said softly. 'That's interesting.' He looked back into Eric's eyes. Then he looked down. 'I would see that my attitude towards time is grandiose.'

He sat back, clearly intrigued and preoccupied. 'I think that for years I have had this idea that I am mega-important in the world and so I have to come through with all the goods. I don't think that logically, obviously, but it's a kind of drive in me, it's how I live, as if I am making the world's most essential contribution at any given moment and must keep on.

'That is obviously stupid. To see myself that way is an act of grandiosity. Funny, too, because I just wrote to a friend about grandiosity. I said that grandiosity and victimization are the same thing, and that if she would give up both, she would be even more accomplished. Odd.'

Eric was dying to comment. The statement about grandiosity and victimization he thought was right, and well-put. But he didn't say so. He could do that later. Instead he asked Kyle again, '*If you knew that you are the only one who does have control over your life, what else would you do to live differently?*'

Kyle said, 'If I knew that I really am the only one who does have control over my life, . . . I would realize that I can accomplish more if I do only what is consistent with my goals and say no to the rest.' He looked away. So Eric did not go on.

'It's funny but I think that by doing too much, I don't do well what matters to me most. So in a funny sort of way, by doing too much I am doing too little.'

Eric smiled and nodded when Kyle looked at him. 'Shall I ask you again?'

'Yeah, good.'

'*If you knew that you are the only one who does have control over your life, what else would you do to live differently?*'

'I would think,' Kyle said immediately, 'about how I really want to live my life. If it were to be a life that made me smile, how would it look? And I would describe it on paper. And then I would meet with my boss and tell her. And then I would play it by ear, I guess. I'd see what she says about it.'

'OK,' Eric said, sparkling but not commenting, 'I'll ask you again: *If you knew that you do have control over your life, what else would you do to live differently?*' He was sure that by now this question would sound stale to Kyle.

'Well, I would think about how I would like Nicole to be living in twenty years and try to model that for her. I would also ask Nicole how she would like things to be different for us at home and different for me. She might have some ideas. Kids can think too.'

'Once more?' Eric asked.

'Sure.'

'If you knew that you are the only one who does have control over your life, what else would you do to live differently?'

Kyle's eyes scanned the room. 'I think I would start a task force in this company and call it "Living For a Change" and ask people in smallish groups to think of every idea, wacky or sane, to change the way this company operates so that people can have a life. And I would include in that people who could think about the quarterly profits issue too. And strategic thinkers, you know, to consider how changes would affect the company's success ten years from now.' He smiled.

'Again?' Eric asked.

'Once more,' Kyle said.

'If you knew that you are the only one who does have control over your life, what else would you do to live differently?'

'I would this afternoon take thirty minutes, speed-read my e-mail and then send CC messages to every department head saying that they are not to send me any mail that is not relevant to the four major projects I am in charge of. And I would say no to the Symphony Board and tonight I would sit down. When Nicole comes in from rehearsal, I would smile.'

Eric and Kyle looked at each other. Eric opened his mouth, but before he could speak Kyle said. 'No more questions.'

'Are you sure?' Eric said lightly.

'Yeah. That's enough. Life looks hopeful. And I'm tired.'

Part 5: Writing It Down

'OK,' said Eric 'Why don't you write down the Incisive Question?'

Kyle reached for his notebook. 'This is the easy part.' He started to write, 'If I had control . . .'

Eric corrected, 'If I knew that I am the only one who does have control . . .'

'Oh, yeah, that's different isn't it? If I knew that *I am the only one who does* have control, what would I do to stop living this way . . .'

'*What would I do to live differently?*' Eric corrected again.

'Yes, that's better.'

'It was your wording,' Eric said.

'Is that why it works?' Kyle looked over at me.

'Yes,' I said. 'Your words are perfect for you.'

Just below the question Kyle wrote down the ideas he had come up with in the session. He remembered them all. Eric did not need to list them for him.

Part 6: Appreciating Each Other

Kyle closed his notebook and looked back at Eric. He said, 'Thanks. That was amazing. Not just in this session but all the time you are respectful of people, encouraging of them. That makes you a damn good manager.'

'Thank you,' said Eric, resisting the urge to resist the compliment. He said, 'And I admire your willingness to face off the lions. You do that day after day.'

'Thanks,' said Kyle, also resisting resisting.

Eric smiled and nodded and then asked Kyle, 'How many times do you think I asked the Incisive Question?'

'Three times?' Kyle said.

'Six,' said Eric.

Kyle looked over at me and shook his head. 'I didn't notice. That's amazing.'

'I know,' I said. 'As long as the question generates new ideas, the question itself is new.'

Eric said, 'That session was obviously good for Kyle. But it was equally as good for me. I don't mean just as the Thinking Partner, though it was. I enjoyed it. But for *me*, another pathologically over-booked person. I can see that the workload boil might get lanced this way. I'll think about it too some time. Thanks. And put me on the task force. The commitment to end over-commitment. Great.'

CHAPTER 26

Thinking Session Part 1: What Do You Want to Think About?

In the presence of the question, the mind thinks again.

Alice, manager in a large UK charity, said, 'Part 1 of the session is the point; the other parts are a last resort.'

This comment was disturbing to people at first because it challenged the excitement, the near magic, produced by Parts 2, 3 and 4 of the Thinking Session. People like to find the limiting assumption and then to see it vanish with that gleamingly accurate 'If you knew . . .' Incisive Question. The polish of it draws them.

However, Alice was right. The real point of a Thinking Session *is* Part 1: to help people think for themselves without obstruction. Part 1 is the open, free-flying time for the Thinker to explore a topic of their choice. Because they are not interrupted or steered by the Thinking Partner, they nearly always have new insights, they find answers to questions, they see order in disorder, they have brand-new ideas they did not suspect were in them and they face things they had not dared face. They sometimes even resolve the issue they brought to the session. They think more clearly. The other parts exist in case Part 1 does not deliver the goods.

What Does the Thinking Partner Do?

Uninvaded time is what people need first in order to think for themselves. They need a turn of their own. They need quiet. They need permission to keep going, attention of the highest order, understanding and encouragement to be as intelligent as they truly are. As their Thinking Partner you can provide all of these things.

You can spin an enticing fibre of respect from the filaments of your interest and your ease, from the steady respect in your eyes and from the nods and murmurings of understanding you utter. They will think boldly, wrapped in this quality of attention.

When they pause, if they pause enveloped still in their thoughts, just be. Stay still and fascinated. Lean back into their quiet. They are busy. They will shortly speak again.

Is There Anything More?

If, however, they pause and say with their eyes or with words that they have finished, be prepared now to intervene.

The first thing to do is not to assume that they are finished. It is very likely that they are just detained for the moment by a limiting assumption. They have begun to assume that they should stop, that you don't want to hear more, that perhaps they are not intelligent enough to think about this after all, that they have just been wittering, not thinking, and that you are surely bored by now.

They need only the barest nudge to continue. There is more, often much more, forming itself to be matured and spoken even in those partial seconds between the stopping and the encouragement to continue. But don't *tell* them to continue, *ask* them. Ask them this question: 'Is there anything more you think or feel or want to say?' Their minds will almost always walk forwards with more ideas, grateful for the invitation. In the presence of the question, the mind thinks again.

That question 'Is there anything more?' is so precise, so keen. It dispels the assumptions that had limited and stopped the Thinker. It opens the mind again to itself.

You may be reluctant to ask it. It may seem to you a stupid question.

Why, if the Thinker just said that was all, would you ask them if there is anything more? Won't they then suspect you were not listening to them? No: the Thinker does not register the question as stupid but as permission to keep thinking. The assumption that they should stop has been dismissed and they find more they want to say. When they stop again, ask again – the same question, 'Is there anything more you think or feel or want to say?'

Only when they say no definitively, only when they do not elaborate, do you agree to stop. And even then you might just ask gently, 'Are you sure?' Occasionally that last chance to say more can be the exact point of safety needed for the Thinker to form and expose not only another idea but sometimes even the core idea they had not, until this moment, been willing to venture.

When they are *certain* they have nothing else to say, Part 1 is over. As the Thinking Partner you do not analyse it or comment on it; you don't even praise it. You just let it be.

Summary of Behaviour Guidelines for the Thinking Partner

- Pay unbelievably beautiful attention to the Thinker, even if you don't agree with them or like them.
- When you are listening, keep your eyes on their eyes. Don't look away unless there is a fire or you have a seriously unsavoury personal emergency.
- Look interested; or rather *be* interested.
- Make sounds only occasionally to indicate understanding and encouragement.
- Be at ease. Nothing horrible is about to happen.
- Smile occasionally, when it won't be interpreted as derision.
- Don't even think about interrupting.
- Don't ask picky clarifying or confirming questions unless you are so confused that you feel faint.

- When your partner has nothing more to say, ask: 'What more do you think or feel or want to say about this?'
- Again, do not even think about interrupting them.
- If the Thinker becomes quiet, but their eyes are alive, relax. *They are still thinking.* Leave them to it. The fact that they are not talking does not mean they are not thinking.

What Does the Thinker Need Now?

After Part 1 the Thinker needs to focus. They need to decide what more, if anything, they want from the session now. You don't figure out for them what they want to achieve. That is their job. To do it for them would infantilize them. And what you suggest would most likely be wrong: it would be your guess, not their idea.

Just ask. 'What do you want the session to achieve at this point?' If they are not satisfied, if they want more, they will say. That is why Parts 2, 3 and 4 were constructed. They appear only when Part 1 is not enough. They are, as Alice said, a last resort. But they do blaze.

CHAPTER 27

Thinking Session Part 2: What Do You Want to Achieve?

To determine someone else's goal for them is an act of infantilization.

There couldn't be a simpler question than that which opens Part 2: 'What do you want the session to achieve at this point?' But be prepared to wait for the answer. This question in itself is a gold mine for the Thinker.

First, it gives the Thinker hope. Having made gains from their thinking in Part 1, but not yet having resolved the issue to their satisfaction, they are not being allowed to give up or be discouraged. The opening question implies that more is possible. The inclusion in it of the words *'at this point'* acknowledges that they have already achieved important things.

Second, the Thinker will now have to organize and prioritize their thoughts. They will have to figure out what they really *do* want the session to achieve now. Often the Thinker has come to the session with many related issues and unsolved problems, and they don't really know which is most important or accessible from all of it. To focus is a challenge. It is, however, an empowering challenge. They have an opportunity here to sort through the issues without cynicism or blame. They are in charge of the outcome of the session and they have to think hard about which outcome they want. They have to take themselves seriously. They cannot see themselves as a victim. They are leading.

What Does the Thinking Partner Do Now?

As the Thinking Partner you want to keep in mind several things:

- There are many blocks to thinking. Part 1 removes most of them. These blocks are:

  a) Poor attention. In Part 1 the Thinking Partner provides high-quality attention, ease, appreciation, encouragement, equality, all of which remove blocks to thinking.

  b) Poor-quality information. The Thinking Partner can sometimes supply full, accurate information. Otherwise the session stops until the Thinker can find high-quality information elsewhere.

  c) Bad feelings. In Part 1 the Thinker is encouraged to release painful emotion such as anger, grief and fear. Crying, for example, is considered an intelligent activity in a Thinking Session.

  d) Physical discomfort. Ideally the Thinking Session should begin only when the Thinker is physically comfortable and when the place is set up to say back to the Thinker, 'You matter.'

- What the Thinker wants the session to achieve at this point would already have been achieved in Part 1 with this exception: something was in their way that the features of Part 1 could not remove.

- The remaining block to thinking after Part 1 is virtually always a limiting assumption.

- Before you can find that assumption, you have to know what the assumption is blocking – that is, you have to know what the Thinker's goal of the session is now.

- So listen with precision. Hear *exactly* the words of the Thinker.

Why Not Paraphrase?

We are taught to paraphrase. We are told that paraphrasing something makes it and us more sophisticated. It shows we are clever. It shows we have heard the speaker and can improve on what they have said. It gives us a role.

For years I assumed that paraphrasing was the right thing to do. But close observation of a person in the face of an Incisive Question reveals that paraphrasing weakens the impact of the question. We are saying, by paraphrasing, that we think they should use our wording. That is more infantilization.

In Thinking Environment work paraphrasing, analysing, interpreting and labelling are not indications of cleverness. They are signs you have not been listening astutely enough. The best wording is the Thinker's own: their mind has specifically chosen and uttered those exact words for a reason. Those words mean something to the Thinker. They come from somewhere and are rich with the Thinker's history, culture, experience and any number of associations in the Thinker's life. They are the words which, when put in the Incisive Question, will work. Your words, however charming or erudite, will not work as beautifully. So you don't have to go to the trouble of changing the Thinker's words. Just remember them.

Don't feel bad if you suddenly realize you've forgotten them. This is not a performance; it is a partnership. So just ask, 'Tell me again what it is that you want the session to achieve,' and listen better this time. It doesn't hurt the Thinker to say it again. Sometimes repeating it even refines it further.

And if the Thinker states the goal in a long, long sentence or paragraph, listen to it all and then ask them to put it in fewer words. Remember: the goal as stated will appear at the end of the Incisive Question, and you really can't be doing with an Incisive Question that ends in fifty-seven words. Do not succumb to the urge to shorten it on the Thinker's behalf, for once again you will have infantilized them.

Remember Chapter 4? The goal was 'to talk to Neil'. Simple enough; don't embellish it. Don't change it to 'have a conversation with your chief executive' just to look active. Remembering the Thinker's exact words is the impressive way to be active here.

CHAPTER 28

Thinking Session Part 3: What Are You Assuming?

**The most tenacious block
to new ideas
is a limiting assumption.**

Between the Thinker and their goal is a *limiting assumption*. Replacing it with a freeing assumption will give the mind access to ideas not reachable before. But you have to find the assumption first. That is what the Thinker needs now in order to keep thinking. That is the purpose of Part 3.

As always, the Thinker finds the assumption. You just ask – and listen. You may *think* you already know what their limiting assumption is, but the Thinker knows more about their own assumptions than anyone else.

Part 3 in Action

So, after listening in Part 1 and determining the Thinker's goal in Part 2, ask: 'What might you be assuming that is stopping you from achieving your session goal?'

Then wait. The Thinker will know. And when they answer, listen again, all the way through all of the assumptions. Ask them what else they might be assuming that is stopping them from achieving their goal, and listen some more.

When they have no more assumptions to reveal, ask them to choose the one that is most in their way. As in every other part, you do not figure that out for them. They will figure it out more accurately than you can if you ask them, 'Of these assumptions which do you think is limiting you most?' You don't even have to recap all the assumptions. In fact, please don't. The Thinker does not need to hear all of their assumptions again just so you can prove that you were listening. They simply need to be asked which is the most poisonous one. In the presence of the question they will know.

Now listen very carefully. When they say the key assumption, get every word right, just as you did with their goal. Ask them to shorten it (don't do it for them) if it is cumbersome (more than ten words or so) and then memorize it. That done, this is what you will have:

- their goal;
- their key assumption.

You are now ready to construct the Incisive Question. To do so all you need is the goal and the assumption. Then the magic can begin – almost.

Facts, Possible-facts and Bedrock Assumptions

There is one more thing. The Thinker will articulate one of *three kinds of assumptions*. You have to determine which kind it is. It will be one of the following:

- a fact ('I am not the boss; he is');
- a possible-fact ('The boss might laugh at me or think I am stupid');
- a bedrock assumption about the self ('I am stupid') or about how life works ('It is not all right to get it wrong').

Facts

Facts are obvious. They are objective. They are not subjective perceptions. You are not the boss: that is a fact. No argument.

Possible-facts

Possible-facts are also fairly obvious. They, like facts, are not subjective, and they are usually about events or circumstances or about what other people might say or do. It is not definite that they will, but they might. The boss might laugh at me and he might think I am stupid. True, he might. That is a possible-fact.

Bedrock Assumptions

However, there is a deeper level of assumptions that is *subjective*. They are rock in the mind, ancient deposits that stop its flow. They were made without our permission a long time ago. They came from many directions and seemed like reality. These I call limiting bedrock assumptions. They are hard core and dangerous.

For a long time, after distinguishing between a possible-fact and a bedrock assumption, we thought there was only one kind of bedrock assumption. We thought it was always about the *self* ('I am stupid, I am bad, I am powerless'). But eventually we began to notice some were about *how life works*, not about the self. These have become revered lore and people defend them fiercely ('It is not all right to get it wrong,' 'It isn't possible,' 'You can never trust people' and 'Because the experts haven't figured it out, I can't' are some favourites).

You need to recognize 'life' assumptions as bedrock just as decisively as you recognize 'self' assumptions as bedrock. Both are slowly dripped into us throughout our growing-up. We hear both everywhere we turn, from family stories, from music, from people, from film, from print, from games, from art, from graffiti, from history. Both kinds are untrue and limiting.

What Is True and What Isn't? – The Positive Philosophical Choice

But how do I know for sure that 'I am stupid' and 'It is not all right to get it wrong?' are untrue?

I don't; not for sure. I don't know anything for sure. I can't prove it. I cannot even prove that I exist or that you do. We all *agree* that I exist and that you exist, but we cannot absolutely prove it. So we have to choose. We have to make a philosophical choice about what is and is not true about the nature of life and the nature of the human being.

I chose a *positive* philosophical view of human nature and of life. I chose it not because it is pleasant and kind or because it was the premise of my counselling training and the basic tenet of Quakerism. I chose it because it works – it keeps people thinking well for themselves. The negative philosophical choice does not work. For the purposes of thinking for ourselves the observably more productive philosophical choice about what is true about human beings and about how life works is a positive one. If you choose to assume that you are enterprising and bright, you will think more clearly and with more colour and precision than you will if you choose to assume that you are stupid.

Just try it. Let me ask you, 'If you knew that you are stupid and that it is not all right to get it wrong, how would you talk to your boss?' Wake me when you have thought of something – if I am not dead by then.

But if I said to you, 'If you knew that you are intelligent and that it is all right to get it wrong, how would you talk to your boss?' you would have interesting ideas. And you would find the courage to act on them.

The human mind thinks for itself best when making a positive philosophical choice about the self and about how life works, when choosing to assume that humans by nature are inherently good, intelligent, powerful, full of choice, loving, loveable, able and alive. If you choose a negative view, the Thinker will continue to be unable to think further. If you choose a positive philosophical view, you will be of enormous help. The person's thinking will sail again. The positive philosophical choice is a pragmatic one.

Sample Assumptions
Over the years we have collected hundreds of assumptions people make

that stop them from thinking well and from taking action. You may recognize a few of the most common ones:

Possible-fact Assumptions

- They might think I am stupid.
- They might laugh.
- They might say no.
- They might select someone else.
- They might marginalize me.
- It might fail.
- They do not care about this as much as I do.
- It will be difficult.
- I might cry.
- Things will never be the same again.
- Nothing will change anyway.

Limiting Bedrock Assumptions: Perceptions of Self

- I am stupid.
- I do not have a right to say what I think.
- I am not worthy of good outcomes.
- My ideas do not matter.
- I cannot handle it.
- I am trapped. I have no choice. I have no power.
- My feelings do not count.
- I cannot make a difference.
- I am not loveable.
- I am not attractive the way I am.
- It is up to me to make everyone's life right.
- I cannot lead.

Limiting Bedrock Assumptions: How Life Works

- It is not all right to get it wrong.
- I have to have all the answers.
- It isn't possible.
- Change is always difficult and takes a long time.
- Because the experts haven't figured it out, I can't.
- What doesn't kill you makes you stronger.
- Competition between people leads to excellence.
- People like me are not important.
- People in power think best.
- Certainty is achievable.
- The way to prevent disaster is to be constantly vigilant.
- Acknowledging your successes precipitates decline.
- Peace is always better than honesty.
- Talking about a problem means you are weak.
- Listening puts you in a vulnerable position.
- If it is mostly for *you*, you have no right to do it.
- Ordinary people cannot affect large social systems.
- You can't have it both ways.
- People don't leave Laguna Beach.

(Let me say a word about Laguna Beach. I was coaching a woman who wanted to make a career change. Her goal for the session was to figure out what she *really* wanted to do. Most of her preferred choices were outside her town of Laguna Beach.

'What are you assuming,' I asked her, 'that is stopping you from figuring out what you really want to do?'

'I am assuming that people just don't leave Laguna Beach,' she said. With a straight face.

Well, that is ridiculous, I thought. Of course people leave Laguna Beach. In fact most of the world has never even heard of Laguna Beach. I don't care how warm the sun is there. But I didn't say that with the wild amazement I felt. I just asked, 'If you knew that people do leave Laguna Beach, what would you really want to do next in your career?'

I was shocked at the instant relief and liberation that came over her face. She really, really had been assuming that people in their right minds don't leave Laguna Beach, that it is the best place on earth to work and live and that leaving is a kind of life-quality, work-opportunity suicide. But in the face of the Incisive Question, she figured out exactly what she wanted to do next in her career. That had simply not been clear to her until that moment. So I kept quiet about this woman and her truly weird assumption.

Then, about a year later, I was coaching someone from Oxford University. He wanted to change his work from an academic life to publishing.

'What are you assuming,' I asked, 'that is stopping you from changing from academic life to publishing?'

'I am assuming that people just don't leave Oxford.'

Hmmm.

Then, working with a solicitor, I heard, 'I am assuming that people in their right mind just don't leave Jacobson and Wilke.'

Well, I apologize. That assumption is as embedded and widespread and limiting as any others. I then could not resist putting it on the list.)

Why Distinguish?
Whether the Thinker's assumption is a possible-fact or a bedrock assumption determines what question you ask next.

Finding the Bedrock Assumption
In a Thinking Partnership (as opposed to a business meeting) you are

usually looking for the bedrock assumption. It is the core culprit blocking the Thinker's next thoughts. It is also the force that can prevent the
Thinker from taking action, so it is worth the search.

Sometimes as the Thinking Partner you get lucky. You listen beautifully through Part 1, asking when appropriate if there is anything more
the Thinker thinks or feels about the topic. You make sure there is
nothing more.

Then you move into Part 2 and ask them what they want the session
to achieve at this point. They tell you their session goal succinctly and
you remember it correctly.

Then with hardly a flutter you move to Part 3 and ask, 'What are you
assuming that is stopping you from achieving your session goal?' They
say, 'I am assuming that I am stupid.' You ask yourself, 'Is that a possible-
fact or a bedrock assumption?' You see right away that that is an untrue
subjective perception of self, a limiting bedrock assumption.

You then move into Part 4 by beginning to construct an Incisive
Question that will remove the assumption and replace it with a freeing
one.

Smooth enough.

The Bedrock Search Question

But sometimes you don't get lucky. Sometimes the Thinker's first answer
to 'What are you assuming?' is not a bedrock assumption. Sometimes it
is a fact or a possible-fact. The Thinker might answer, 'They might laugh
at me.' That is a possible-fact. If you remove it and say, 'If you knew that
they might *not* laugh at you,' the Thinker will only partly believe you.
You wish they had said a bedrock assumption. But they didn't. So what
do you do to find the bedrock assumption?

That juncture tangled me up for ages. I couldn't figure out why the
Thinker was allowing the possible-fact to stop them. To me the
Thinker's possible-fact assumption was a nothing issue. Privately I

wanted to say (and I think we often do say this sort of thing to people half the time), 'Who cares if they laugh at you? Are you going to let that keep you from doing what you want and need to do?' To us, the people who live outside another person's assumption, the threat of the possible-fact is nothing. *Inside* the assumption, however, the person is immobilized. So the Thinker experiences my question as impatience and reproach from me, not as encouragement to think.

It finally occured to us that something was *making* that possible-fact assumption stop them from thinking. What could be so strong, we wondered, that could make a mere possible-fact grind a human mind to a halt?

Not suprisingly, but after a surprisingly long period of more research, we saw that underneath the possible-fact assumption was a limiting bedrock assumption. The challenge then was to find it. What question could we ask that could seek out and identify that bedrock assumption beneath the possible-fact?

Designing the question took ages. Indefatigable, not to say driven, we finally came up with the awkward but powerful wording: 'That's possible. But what are you assuming that makes that stop you?' This question slides beneath the possible-fact and captures the bedrock culprit.

The next step, removing that bedrock assumption, would, by comparison, be simple.

CHAPTER 29

Thinking Session Part 4: If You Knew . . .

> Limiting assumptions
> can be removed
> with an Incisive Question.

What the Thinker needs now in order to keep thinking is to get rid of the limiting assumption and to find ideas on the other side.

Part 4 of the Thinking Session – that moment people say they like best in this model, that laser-like process of asking the Incisive Question and then watching the explosion of creativity for the Thinker that occurs a second later – seems effortless when you see it done well. But constructing the Incisive Question takes unbelievable precision.

As always, you don't help the Thinker to this place beyond the block by just telling them to go there. You don't say, 'So you are assuming you are stupid. Well, that's dumb. So stop assuming that and tell me what new ideas you have about your goal.' That won't work. That command requires obedience and, again, the human mind wants not to obey. It wants to think.

To do this it needs questions. The question this time is a kind of game. It creates a new reality for the Thinker. It hypothesizes a 'new knowing', a different reality, that does not contain the limiting assumption.

Finding the Positive Opposite

First you have to make sure you know exactly how to *word the freeing assumption* that will replace the limiting one. As always you look to the Thinker to find the words.

You know her assumption: I am stupid. So why not just take that assumption, replace it with its opposite, put it into a question, connect it with the goal of the session and varoom – new thinking.

I did exactly that for several years. 'If you knew that you are not stupid, what would you do in this situation?'

This process worked well enough – sort of. If I am honest, it was kind of sluggish. It didn't quite let the Thinker's mind soar because 'not stupid' is only so-so in its positive impact. It is definitely a back door.

One day the Thinker pointed that out to me. I said, 'OK, how about "clever". If you knew that you are clever, what would you do?' That was better. But it still wasn't quite it. She wasn't satisfied. More alarming, she also wasn't having any particularly good ideas from the question.

I was mildly annoyed, but successfully suppressing it. Then a thought – ask the Thinker.

'Well,' I said, 'what do *you* think would be the right word?'

She thought for a moment. I figured she would say 'clever' after all, or 'intelligent', perhaps. I was waiting, but not fascinated.

'Intriguing,' she said.

Intriguing? I thought. That is not the opposite of stupid, is it?

Apparently. For her. The positive opposite of stupid, in that Thinking Session at that particular moment with that particular woman, seemed to be 'intriguing'.

Who was I to argue? Now I *was* fascinated.

So I asked her, 'If you knew that you are intriguing, what would you do in this situation?' And I can tell you one thing: from the quality and diversity of the ideas she thought of from that question, intriguing is definitely the opposite of stupid.

So I now systematically ask the Thinker before I construct the Incisive Question to tell me what *their* positive opposite of that word would be. And I use it. No argument. With hardly an exception the Thinker's word is fresher, more accurate for them, more exactly right, than any I would have thought of.

A truly startling example of this positive opposite principle at work occurred in a session a year later. The Thinker had said, 'I want to feel confident around Sam. But I am assuming that he is better than I am in almost everything.' The Thinking Partner started to say, 'If you knew that Sam is not better than you are . . . ,' but she stopped herself and asked, 'What is your positive opposite of "he is better than I am in every way"?'

The Thinker looked away. Then suddenly her face opened and her eyes danced. She turned back to the Thinking Partner and said, 'I am blindingly stunning in every way.'

Wow. It is always worth the asking. She says that the ideas and action from that accurately, uniquely worded Incisive Question have been continuous and good.

Designing the Incisive Question

Designing the Incisive Question requires the twin masteries of memory and simplicity. First, you must remember what the Thinker has said their assumption is, in their *exact* words. Then, when applicable, you must remember what their phrase is for the positive opposite of their assumption, again in their words.

The Incisive Question does one thing and does it expertly. It removes the barrier that is stopping the person from thinking further. 'If you knew . . .' questions are the most common. For example, 'If you knew that you are blindingly stunning in every way, how would you feel around Sam?' In that format you are removing the assumption in the first part and asking for ideas towards the session goal in the second part.

That question is called 'incisive' because it cuts cleanly into the assumption, making a finely placed incision, and removes it. It leaves in its place a new, freeing assumption, a truth based on a positive philosophical choice. And suddenly the thinking of the person is released. New ideas seem to come from nowhere. The Incisive Question is precise, carefully and logically formed, and exactly reflects the Thinker's issue, goal, assumption and wording. The results of the Incisive Question are worth all the attention and effort that led to it. It is the discipline of the wording that leads to the freedom of thinking.

At last the Thinker gets to find more ideas. They get on the other side of the thinking barrier, the bedrock assumption, and sometimes they see life differently. It is here in Part 4, as well as in Part 1, that both the Thinking Partner and the Thinker witness the inimitable beauty of thinking for yourself.

To construct an Incisive Question:

1 Hypothesize ('If you knew . . . .').
2 Follow with a freeing true assumption ('. . . that you are blindingly stunning . . .').
3 Attach that new assumption to the goal ('. . . how would you feel around Sam?').

The full questions is: 'If you knew that you are blindingly stunning in every way, how would you feel around Sam?

If you knew + *freeing assumption* + *goal* = Incisive Question.

That is about as computational as I am willing to get with this dance of a process. But it really is that sleek.

After the complexities of

1 hearing the assumption,
2 figuring out which kind of assumption it is,
3 searching for the bedrock assumption beneath any possible-fact,

4 finding out the Thinker's positive opposite of a limiting assumption, and then

5 designing the Incisive question to remove it,

you as their Thinking Partner can, once again, sit back and watch the elegance.

Ask It Again

Ask the Incisive Question once and you will hear one idea. Ask it again and you will hear another. But don't stop there. Ask it again: the *exact same* question. And surprise yourself at how readily the Thinker comes up with yet another idea. Each one is different, even in kind, from the other. Ask it yet again.

The Thinker will not notice how many times the Incisive Question is asked. And the repetition of it will not be repetitious to them. As long as it releases a fresh idea, it is a fresh question.

Eventually the Thinker will not want the question again. No more new ideas will flow from the question. That is a natural stopping place. You do not have to decide for the Thinker when to stop. Either they or the clock will do that job.

Tense

In the Incisive Question use the *present tense* when stating the new positive truth. For example, 'If you knew that you *are* blindingly stunning' is a different question from 'If you knew that you *were* blindingly stunning.' The present tense states a truth. The past tense (technically the subjunctive tense) states a hypothesis.

The difference matters because the Incisive Question takes its power from stating a new, positive, chosen *truth* about the Thinker or about how life works.

The hypothetical parts of the Incisive Question are in the first three words, 'If you knew', and in the last clause asking for ideas about the goal of the session, 'what would change for you in this situation?' Those verbs are hypothetical because you are just supposing. You are not commanding the Thinker to believe it. You are just enticing them into a moment of almost playful speculation.

The fact that the knowing is hypothetical allows them to play with the new truth and not get defensive or resistant as they might if you gave the new truth to them as a command. The hypothetical tense in the last clause allows them to think imaginatively beyond fear of commitment to act. Action follows best when it is first seen as a possibility, not as a requirement.

Removing Facts and Possible-facts

The discussion so far of Parts 3 and 4 of the session has focused on the search for and removal of the deepest-level assumption, the bedrock assumption. When you remove a limiting bedrock assumption and replace it with a freeing, more productively true one, you have a tool that will apply to more issues than just the one you focused on in your session. 'If I knew that I am intelligent . . .' will apply to hundreds of situations. 'If I knew that the boss might not think I am stupid . . .', on the other hand, will apply only to the particular situation with the boss.

'I am intelligent' is also a dependable chosen philosophical view of the self, true forever, whereas 'the boss might not think I am stupid' is entirely dependent on the boss's views of you at a given moment, not on an eternal view of human nature. 'The boss might not think I am stupid' is, therefore, less likely to keep you thinking afresh because you can justifiably collapse into the haunting possibility that the boss does think you are stupid. If you can't find out directly from her, you will sustain the doubt. 'If I knew that the boss might not think I am stupid' may give you some good ideas, but it will not dependably give you the confidence to act on them. You will soon revert to the converse possibility that she does think you are stupid. That is why I encourage people to seek and remove the bedrock assumption.

However, exploration of that sort is too deep, requiring too much safety, to occur in most work situations. So it is at the level of facts and possible-facts that most people at work remove assumptions. And creating those Incisive Questions is very simple, much less intricate than finding the accurate bedrock assumption and creating the precise Incisive Question to remove it.

To remove a fact, for example, merely hypothesize its opposite. Fact: 'I am not the chief executive.' Incisive Question: 'If I were the chief executive, I would . . .' Fact: 'I am not a woman.' Incisive Question: 'If I were a woman in this situation, I would . . .' Fact: 'I am afraid.' Incisive Question: 'If I were not afraid, I would . . .' These questions open the mind to all kinds of new possibilities. Ideas flow even from allowing the fact to be an assumption for a few minutes and replacing it with one that digs the mind out of powerlessness and lethargy.

The same is true for a possible-fact assumption. Simply hypothesize its opposite. But use a tentative tense in order to respect the negative possibility too. Possible-fact: 'The boss might think I am stupid.' Incisive Question: 'If I knew that the boss might not think I am stupid, I would . . .' Possible-fact: 'I might alienate everyone.' Incisive Question: 'If I knew there is a chance I will interest some of them, I would . . .' Possible-fact: 'I might get fired . . .' Incisive Question: 'If I thought I might even get promoted, I would . . .'

These new assumptions, replacing the limiting ones, are easy to formulate. And they do produce new ideas. But they do not precisely identify and remove the assumption, which makes the facts and possible-facts have power over you. Thus they are effective less long, less widely, and provide you with less courage. They are, however, magic in settings where ideas are dull and safety is minimal. They are wondrous at work.

Don't Ask

A colleague rang me and said, 'I was coaching my client. I asked him the Incisive Question and it didn't work. He did not have any ideas. So I asked him again and it still didn't work. I changed my tone but he still had no ideas. What did I do wrong?'

I asked Barbara what her client's goal for the session was.

'To understand why he can't sustain success.'

Ah – to understand. That is why the Incisive Question did not work.

When the Thinker's session goal is 'to understand or to find out why' about something in them, that goal will be met in Part 3. There is no need for Part 4. Just ask, 'What are you assuming that stops you from sustaining success?' The assumption the Thinker discovers will be the answer to 'why' that they were looking for. In fact most of the whys about our behaviour are the assumptions on which that behaviour was based in the first place.

Barbara's client had not asked to have these assumptions removed. He just wanted to find them so that he would understand his behaviour. He discovered his assumption that 'people like him are not important'. That assumption was preventing his sustaining success.

But when Barbara then removed it with the Incisive Question, 'If you knew that people like you *are* important, what would you do?', she was going beyond what he had asked for. She had decided *for him* that he should go on to Part 4.

The question generated resistance and no new ideas. The stopping power of infantilization is not to be underestimated.

So listen carefully in Part 2 to determine *what sort of goal it is.* If it is a knowing, understanding, finding-out-why kind of a goal, stop after Part 3.

Go back then to Part 2 and ask, 'Now what would you like the session to achieve?' If they want to remove the assumption just found in

Part 3, they will say so. If they don't, the session is over. You will not have infantilized them by deciding for them. And if they choose to go on, Part 4 will be superb.

Silent Incisive Questions

One more thing about Incisive Questions. They are not always verbal. This became clear to us when someone asked, 'If it is true that Incisive Questions are what remove blocks in a Thinker's mind and allow for ideas to emerge, why does Part 1 of the session work so well when we are not asking any Incisive Questions there?'

That puzzle lasted a while. Then one day it dawned on us. Part 1 is actually a whole series of *silent* Incisive Questions. Asking general Incisive Questions is actually what the Thinking Partner is doing when they appear to being doing so little. Without a word they are asking the questions that second by second keep the most prevalent bedrock assumptions, the ones that stop people from thinking out loud for themselves, at bay.

With their attentive, respectful behaviour, they are silently asking the Thinker questions like these:

- If you knew that you can think about this very well, . . .
- If you knew that I respect you as a Thinker, . . .
- If you knew that you are good and worthy of good outcomes, . . .
- If you knew that I am not judging you or evaluating you, . . .
- If you knew that I will not interrupt you, . . .
- If you knew that you are in charge of this session, . . .
- If you knew that I will be confidential with everything you say, . . .
- If you knew that people from your background can think brilliantly, . . .
- If you knew that you can come up with ideas that are better than mine, . . .

. . . what would you think and say next?

With your attention – with your eyes, your face, the tone in your voice, in your ease and quiet, in your posture of respect and appreciation – you as the Thinking Partner are asking all of those Incisive Questions and more. Incisive Questions remove limiting assumptions. Sometimes they are spoken; sometimes they are not. In either form they conceive.

CHAPTER 30

Thinking Session Part 5:
Writing It Down

The Incisive Question
is often too accurate to remember.

The Incisive Question is elusive. While you are asking it, it seems engraved, seared into the mind of both of you forever. You cannot believe while you are repeating the question for the fifth or sixth time that the Thinker could ever forget it.

But they probably will. The Incisive Question moves earth, shifts rock and flattens structures everywhere. It forces out of the way assumptions that have been entrenched for decades. Until its new freeing assumption becomes the dominant point of view, rather than the rebel upstart, the old assumptions will, as it were, try to dismantle it, shove it aside, cause the Thinker to misplace it. It is not unusual for the Thinker to get it wrong even a minute after the last asking. They begin to write it down and distort it.

The point of Part 5 of the Thinking Session is to ensure that the Incisive Question does not get lost. Very often that same question is useful again and again, from one situation to another. Some people even keep a book of Incisive Questions that have worked for them and go back to them to use again or to see the irrelevance of them later after significant change has occurred that now makes the questions obsolete.

Part 5 is also a time to write down ideas for action that the Incisive Question has produced. Some people like to do this, others don't. It is not a big deal. Some sessions lead to 'action items' and some don't. For example, if the goal of your session is to *feel* different, there obviously will be no ideas for action. There will just be new feelings already in place, nothing to record.

Think of Part 5 as secretarial. It is usually quick. But it is important to get the Incisive Question on paper before it fades.

CHAPTER 31

Thinking Session Part 6: Appreciation

**Closing with appreciation
keeps people thinking
after the session.**

At the end of the session both the Thinker and the Thinking Partner, to keep thinking for themselves beyond the session, need to hear and give appreciation. The Thinker can easily be assuming, now that the session is over, that the Thinking Partner is having second thoughts about everything they heard, that the Partner now sees the Thinker as weak, disturbed, flaky, any number of unworthy things. Similarly the Thinking Partner can well be assuming that they did not do as good a job as they should have (however brilliant they were – such is the power of self-doubt) and that possibly the Thinker is disappointed in them. So to dispel these assumptions and allow both people to think better as they leave, they appreciate each other, they tell the truth about each other's good qualities.

It is advisable not to refer to the content of the session in this exchange, not to, for example, say, 'Your ideas were excellent' or 'I admire the way you handled the things you described.' It seems at this stage to work best if the appreciation is a simple recognition of a positive quality in the person which is visible outside the session as well as inside: 'I admire the way you take on a challenge' or 'Your encouragement matters to us' – something that does not re-open the session. Referring back to the session content can feel invasive and is infantilizing. Both of you will leave with your mind on the truth of yourselves and each other if you take a second before you leave to mention a quality you respect. The simplicity of this, like so much of a Thinking Environment, belies its power.

Remember also to say 'Thank you', not 'Humph, what would you know?' As I said in Chapter 6, to insult the giver is to destroy the Thinking Environment for you both.

CHAPTER 32

Time Is What It Takes

To take time to think
is to gain time to live.

'I agree this is good. I even agree this is essential. And maybe – no, prob-ably – things would improve in my life and my work if I did it. But I don't have the time. I hardly have time to breathe.'

So runs the most common excuse people give when I suggest they build Thinking Partnerships into their lives. It is weak. Mostly because it is so clamorously illogical.

There is only one thing on which virtually everything else in our lives depends. That is the quality of our thinking. Everything stems from this. Including the passionate bursting of our hearts and the inward non-movements of contemplation. The human being begins each action, each feeling with a thinking process. When that is gone, we are gone. Nothing deserves our care, our time, more than this.

It is this very thing, however, this thing without which we cannot live well, this process of thinking clearly for ourselves, this uniquely human thing, that we can't seem to find time to do. Most of us most of the day do not take time to think for ourselves and we don't pay attention to others well enough for them to do it either. We just go through our days and nights, on and on. We wake tired, we do our jobs, respond to needs (mostly other people's), try to have a little fun, love if we are lucky, and wonder where the time has gone. But we rarely decide to sit down and think. To stop, sit down and think for ourselves, especially with someone paying attention to us expertly, is worth the time it takes. It returns time to us many fold.

I became convinced of the value of taking time like this when I once tracked my activities for a month and found that I spent more time backtracking and correcting the mistakes I had made because I had *not* stopped to think for myself than I would have spent stopping to think in the first place. Some people have told me that they have spent years undoing damage and starting over again because they acted without thinking well first. Fifteen or twenty minutes a day and an hour or so a week doesn't seem like so much when stacked against the hours and days, even years, you spend handling the fall-out from having not taken time to think well beforehand. Mathematically 'I just don't have the time' is not defensible.

Some people have figured this out. They are scheduling short Thinking Sessions first thing in their work day. They set aside thirty minutes to divide with a Thinking Partner, fifteen minutes each, to listen and be listened to. It is no surprise that they report that their day usually goes better and that on occasion they have saved impressive amounts of time because they changed their course of action or decided to move out of passivity or thought of a much more efficient way of doing something or realized that problem obsessing them wasn't a problem after all. They took time to think first and so they did not have to put hours and hours into doing unnecessary things or cleaning up a mess after mounting up mistakes.

Larger, complex issues respond to this practice too. Take the time to think about them clearly and for yourself before you decide what to do, and you will gain time.

Some say that they already do this 'thinking thing' well enough with friends and colleagues, that their ordinary chats are good enough. Then I suggest they actually formalize it, that they each take timed turns and follow the structure of the Thinking Session. Invariably they comment later that it is qualitatively better than the conversations. One is not to replace the other. We need both.

The problem has been that we have the chats, but we don't have the Thinking Sessions. And the problem also has been that in the chats we interrupt each other and take over. The chances of either of us having a seriously new insight or achieving new clarity are very small under those circumstances. So we need to get both into our lives but not confuse the two.

Another reason people put off thinking time is that they believe they already know what they will say, that the time spent will yield nothing new or worthwhile. But we do *not* know, on this side of a Thinking Session, or on this side of our turn in a group, what we will think or say when we stop in the presence of someone's exquisite, intelligent attention. Invariably we think things we could not have predicted. A Thinking Environment is dependably that powerful.

Limited Time

Remember also that *you* can determine how much time to set aside. You do not have to be a victim of the other person's needs. Decide how much total time is good for you and split it with your partner.

Similarly, if you have only five minutes when someone pops into your life and asks you to listen to them, say so. (You can think up all kinds of non-exasperated ways to say this like, 'I have a full five minutes and it is all yours' or 'Sure, go ahead, I don't have to leave for five minutes.') Then stick to it. Don't let them go on and on beyond the time you have comfortably. That is dishonest and you will not listen very well to them. You will be thinking about how to get rid of them. It will make you resentful of them. So stick to your own sense of how much time you can allot.

We *can* find time for Thinking Sessions, formally and informally. Surely if we can find time for television, newspapers, sports events, clubbing, drinks parties and worry, we can find time to think. We need to value our own minds enough to put time to think into our diaries, to be willing to build other things around it. Those other things will be better, richer, smarter as a result.

We would do well to listen to song writer Judy Small when she says, 'Time is what it takes to build a dream that's worth the while.'

Perhaps the Taoist saying is right also:

> There is so much to do.
> There is so little time.
> We must go slowly.

Taking time to think each day is a personal and professional imperative. The surprising mathematics of this we would do well to remember: to take time to think is to gain time to live.

CHAPTER 33

After Thought

So, now, is this it? Is the uncovering of this Thinking Environment process complete?

Not for a minute. The beauty of any model that reveals a natural process is that the natural process is continuously disclosing itself. That is the nature of discovering what is, as opposed to manufacturing what isn't. Its irrepressible vitality is why the Thinking Session works so well.

To ensure that the process evolves intelligently, you need simply to continue to *notice what is happening*. You need to refuse to see what isn't there. Then, when the next piece appears, you won't miss it.

Part Three

The Thinking Society

CHAPTER 34

Introduction: The Possibilities

A Thinking Environment
is a way of being
in the world.

I would like the whole world to become a Thinking Environment.

I would like people to wake up each morning knowing that they are going to be able to think for themselves without punishment; that they can be logical, eloquent, bold and imaginative; that their ideas count; that other people are going to pay attention to them, appreciate them, be at ease with them, allow them to finish their thoughts and their sentences, help them recognize and remove assumptions that are limiting them, acknowledge them as thinking equals.

I would like people wherever they are to have easy access to information, to live and work in places that say 'You matter', to be rewarded, not for being better than others, but for being truly good.

I would like people to know that to cry is grown up, and that *all* of who they are – every shred of background, group identity, belief and physical body – is acceptable.

I would like each person to be encouraged from a young age to dream, not just an individual dream of achievement and well-being, but also a dream for a just and well-functioning world, and I would like it to be commonplace that people take the time to think each day about how to make their dreams come true.

I would like people not to surrender to the cruel comfort of cynicism.

For all these things to happen some of the monoliths of our society are going to have to operate with slightly different rules – but only slightly. Establishing a Thinking Environment is one of those small changes that has a huge effect. Six of these arenas are: health, schools, politics, love relationships and families. In this section of the book I speculate about how these arenas might look if we could turn them into Thinking Environments.

I believe that if we could establish a Thinking Environment throughout society, we would see the human mind operate at impressive new levels of clarity and humanity. And with that would come dignity and wonder and a toss-your-head-back-into-the-rain kind of joy. Again and again the words of Shirley Edwards of Xerox come to mind: 'A Thinking Environment is not just a theory and set of skills. It is a way of being in the world.'

CHAPTER 35

Health

Health is a direct result
of a Thinking Environment.

'Nancy, they say it is cancer. They say you are going to die. Tell me you are going to live.'

I was saturated with anaesthesia and morphine, but I said it. I was twenty-six. The voice was my husband's. I had just been wheeled into intensive care after exploratory surgery had found highly metastatic ovarian tumours the size of mangoes. Malignant cells had spread to my uterus, bowel, appendix and abdominal lining. The surgeon told my husband and parents I would be lucky to live six weeks.

That was long before I had any idea what a Thinking Environment was. But years later I would extrapolate from those weeks in the hospital some essential components for helping a person think for herself.

From that first minute my then husband Peter had in effect set up a positive Thinking Environment in my own mind. I had felt foolish lying there half-conscious with tubes and needles everywhere, saying over and over, 'I will live, I will live.' I did it mostly for him, I think. Deep down, I was in no doubt. It did not occur to me that I would die. But saying it was re-enforcing. It was also reassuring to me that Peter believed I would live. Had he been in doubt, I would have had a much harder time doing my own thinking and devising a strategy to live. He had begun what would become a consistent environment of five times more hope than fear, five times more belief in me than scepticism, five times more appreciation of me than criticism. He told my whole family how important it was for them to be positive too. He told my friends that they were not welcome in our apartment if they had any doubt about my future. That cut our circle down from thirty to eight.

Throughout that week in the hospital Peter researched every underground, non-medicalized approach to cancer he could find. He read. He talked to strangers (some very strange) and attended a conference in which an eminent Taiwanese doctor whose speciality was ovarian cancer was speaking about his herbal treatment. The next day I woke to find a line of Chinese men shoulder to shoulder around my bed. Dr Chou sat on my bed. Peter introduced him as the ovarian specialist with a herb cure. Dr Chou smiled at me warmly.

Then he looked for a long time into my eyes – really into my eyes, through the pupil, up into the lid, from side to side at the iris, looking for something he never discussed. Then he looked at my tongue and felt my wrist for a long time. I kept wondering if he had got the picture that it was ovarian cancer I had, not glaucoma or tonsillitis or high blood pressure. Finally he folded his hands in his lap and said, 'I can treat you with my herbs, but if you decide no, please do this.' He paused. He said slowly – and I will never forget this – 'Be happy, happy, happy.' Then he and his entourage processed out of my room.

Again, I later realized, there had been a construction of positive hope implanted deeply into my mind. Yes, I thought, I can do that. I can be happy, happy, happy. And I slept.

Two more days went by. One morning before dawn, I heard my hospital room door open. I was too drugged and sleepy even to open my eyes, but in a few seconds I heard a voice in my ear. It said, 'Nancy, this is your Uncle Henry Bennett. You know that I am a gynaecological oncologist. I have flown from Oklahoma to look at your slides. And it is true they are very bad. But I have treated many, many women with cancer like yours. And I want you to know that as many women live who just go home as who take chemotherapy.'

That was all. Then he was gone. I never even saw his face. But he had given me vital information. I remember thinking again, 'Yes, I can do that. I can just go home.' Hope and a semblance of a strategy were building. And again I slept.

In the middle of the night, I felt a kind of peace settle into me. I opened my eyes and looked around. There in the chair near my bed, flown in from Vietnam, was my twin brother Bill. He sat very quietly. He smiled at me and blew me a kiss. I slept again. At dawn he was still there, and all that day and all the next night. 'I love you,' he said. 'You are going to be all right.'

I would find out twenty-two years later that on that first night he had placed his hands on my incision and prayed that God would take the cancer out of my body and let him deal with it. He said that a white swirling light came from nowhere and disappeared into my belly. It frightened him so fiercely that he fell back into the chair. Peace and more sleep and his sweet face are all I remember.

Every day Jean, my counsellor, came to see me. She listened to me cry and talk for an hour every afternoon. When the nurses came in, we would pretend to be just having a chat. When they left, I would cry some more.

Meanwhile Peter was gathering information about food. He was talking to people who had recovered from various terminal cancers by changing their diet. One day he arrived in my hospital room with two full paper bags of groceries and unloaded them into my dresser drawer. There were bottles of things I did not know existed: carrot juice, yoghurts, bean sprouts and mineral water. In 1972 nobody 'like us' in Washington was consuming any of these things.

When my hospital lunch came that day, I thanked the nurse for it. The minute she closed the door, Peter wheeled the hospital lunch tray towards himself, reached into the drawer and set up a small meal for me of carrot juice, plain yoghurt, almonds, baked potato, alfalfa sprouts, orange juice and water. I drank and ate all of those things, not then understanding the food theory behind any of it. Peter ate my hospital lunch and then wheeled the big tray back in front of me. When the nurse arrived to remove it, she looked at the empty bowls and plates and said, 'Good girl.'

The next day my father asked me if I would like to take a walk down the hospital hall to get a little exercise. I put my arm in his and felt his respect and tenderness – and his calm, that was a bit unusual for him. As we strolled along – he strolled, I shuffled – he said to me softly, 'Well, honey, the doctors say you are going to die. What do you think?'

I remember that moment vividly. My own father, no doubt desperate inside at the thought of his red-headed young daughter dying, had asked me what *I* thought. So I really thought about it. It took me a minute or so, but he did not push me or answer for me. We just kept taking steps together. Then I knew. It was almost in a shape, nearly tangible but not texturous, barely formed. 'I don't think so, Daddy,' I said, 'because I have lots to do and I don't think I have even started.' He squeezed my hand and kissed me.

Finally, two days later, the surgeon came in to see me and talked for a long time about the prognosis. He said, 'I can get you into the National Institutes of Health [NIH], into a clinical trials programme of the most advanced chemotherapy in the world. If you take it, you will have a 22 per cent chance of living five years. If you don't, you will probably be dead in six weeks. I strongly recommend that you take the NIH offer.'

By that time I was feeling a bit more bold and aware of other approaches to healing, though conversant with none of them yet. I said, 'Dr Marlow, what will this chemotherapy do to the non-cancerous cells? Is the medicine intelligent? Can it distinguish between the cancer and other things? Will it hurt the healthy things in my body?'

I remember the look on his face. It was the look of an exasperated professor wanting to get on with the lesson, impatient with the student's questions, rushed.

'The medicine will kill every growing cell.'

'Like what?' I asked.

'Like bone marrow and hair.'

'Bone marrow?' I asked. 'What will that do to my immune system?'

'We will give you antibiotics to protect you from infection while you are on the chemo.'

'But doesn't the immune system have something to do with killing off the cancer? Don't I need it?' I was shaking now. I had never asked an authority that many questions before in my life.

'Nancy,' he said, helping me understand thoroughly what the word patronizing meant, 'you would be a fool not to take it. It is your only chance.'

'And my hair?' I asked. 'Will it all fall out?'

'Yes,' he said, 'but if you live, it will grow again.'

To this day I do not know which scared me more, losing my immune system or losing my hair. But I decided a 22 per cent chance of living by that regime was not very high and that I would not do it. I decided that somehow, if I could just think clearly about it, I could, with the help of my family and friends, figure out a systematic non-drug regime and stick to it. I wanted to re-build my immune system and see if that way I could get rid of the cancer myself. So for the next few days I asked myself this question: 'If I knew that my body belongs *only* to me, not to doctors, not to cancer drug clinical trials, not to the worried people around me, what would I do in this situation?'

I reasoned that my body had made the cancer, that it had not just flown in through the window one night, and that by making some important changes in my diet, by counselling and by doing now the work I had hoped to do in the future, by *feeling now* the way I would feel at eighty years old, by being loved, perhaps my body could unmake it. It amused me that there were four Fs in this plan: Food, Feelings, Friends and Future.

So we packed to go home. My mother said she would stay for two weeks and cook for me, no matter what kind of weird food I decided to eat. She was completely supportive of my regime. And when she fixed me a meal of baked potato, carrot juice, bean sprouts, yoghurt and fresh vegetables and fruits, she fixed herself a T-bone steak and chips and sat down with me for lunch. We giggled lots that fortnight. That, too, probably helped to heal my body.

Before I was officially released from the hospital, my team of surgeons and oncologists came to see me. They explained again the importance of my being admitted to NIH and being part of the clinical chemo study. I listened. And when they had finished, I took a deep breath and said, 'I have decided not to take the drug. I have decided to go home, drink carrot juice, cry, start a school, write a book, feel the certainty of my future and be happy, happy, happy. I'll see you in five years.'

'If you do that,' said one of the doctors, 'you will be dead in a month.'

That was twenty-seven years ago.

When I look back on that period in my life, I can see the veins of a Thinking Environment running through every part of it. People believed in me. People appreciated me. They listened to me, paid attention to me as if I mattered very much. They asked me good questions and trusted me to think for myself even in the face of articulate threats of death. They let me cry and laugh and say when I was afraid or angry.

They searched out and gave me complete and accurate information of all sorts, medical and nutritional. They regarded me always as their equal in this job ahead of healing and starting my life over – after I left the hospital I never felt infantilized. And they surrounded me in comfort and physical tenderness and beauty. They sat with me serene and at ease as I faced off that supposed monster called metastatic cancer.

It never seemed like a battle to me. It seemed like the creation inside my body of an environment in which intelligent things could start to happen and where healing would be the result of that.

That was my experience. Others have taken different roads, equally successfully. The important thing was that I was allowed to think *for myself* and to set things up to make sense to *me*.

I now think that our bodies know what they need and that if we listen to them, they will tell us more than we can imagine. If we pay undistracted attention to them and do not slip into denial, they will let us know what changes to make to keep them healthy. They are speaking to us most of the time, but we turn away. We ignore them. Eventually we pay the price for it.

I also think, as Janice Rous does, that much of what strains and breaks down the body is the presence, in a physical form, of limiting bedrock assumptions. In her work called Body Dialogue she helps people identify the assumptions that reside in their bodies and asks them incisive questions to remove them. She touches people with a quality of attention that can free the mind and body to heal. She thinks of her work as the art of creating a Thinking Partnership between mind and body.

One question we can ask ourselves in order to begin this Thinking Partnership for ourselves is, 'What am I assuming that may be hurting my body?' It is not unusual for people to answer something like, 'I am assuming that I am not worth the trouble of taking care of it.' And so we would ask, 'If you knew that you are worth any trouble to care for your body, what would you change about your life right now?' The answers will come, and with them the courage to act.

The Doctor in a Thinking Environment

Five years after that exit from the hospital in Washington I was invited to speak at a conference of internists at NIH. Still disdainful of the medical establishment, I hesitated. Eventually, however, I agreed to go. I climbed those big steps up to the white-columned building on the vast campus of NIH and sat down to await my turn to speak. The first presentation turned my crusty little attitude inside out. The professor said, pointing to a graph the size of my living room, 'We are finding that people who are in charge of their life have less recurrence of this kind of cancer than do people who give over their decisions and care to someone else.' My mind faded out as he became more technical. *In charge* was exactly what I had been. Perhaps they would listen to me after all.

They did – absorbed and respectful, the whole time. When I finished I nearly drowned in the rapids of white coats all wanting to know exactly what kind of carrots they were, how long I had cried, where my school was and how I could generate positive feelings of the future when the present had been clearly so dire. I remember going back down those steps with respect for medical science that had eluded me for five years. I no longer mistrusted all cancer doctors. Some, I could now see, wanted a wide field from which to gather their facts. They had listened.

Today, twenty-seven years later, my GP in England is equally wonderful. She sets up a Thinking Environment every time I visit her. She greets me warmly and without a shred of condescension. She then listens to me without interrupting or stopping me. Even when I take quite a long time to talk, she pays attention to me the whole time. She does not nod too much or look away. I feel respected. That in itself I believe starts the healing process in my body.

She is a competent medical doctor, without question, but her attention and respect are at least as important in her work as is her expertise in state-of-the-art diagnosis and treatment. True, she is still rare in this profession. The norm, according to reports and studies, is for doctors to be detached, hurried, emotionally illiterate and full of self-importance.

They are trained in fact to *think for* the patient. Judith Schott's research shows that health-care professionals are formally trained 'to think on behalf of others'.

When doctors were asked in a study recently to say how long they thought they listened without interruption to their patients during office visits, they said, 'Three minutes.' When those same doctors were observed with patients, they actually averaged a listening time of twenty seconds. When the patients were then allowed to talk without interruption until they had said everything on their mind, their actual talking time was an average of three minutes.

We could extrapolate from this that doctors intuitively know how long they should listen if they want to get the full picture from the patient, but that something keeps them from in fact listening that long. What makes a doctor interrupt or ask questions too soon or guide and lead the patient too early is not different from what makes any of us do the same with our friends, clients or family. We think that to help is only to talk, to ask, to suggest.

Anything more?

In truth, however, to help is to listen. To help is also to say, after the patient has finished, 'Is there anything more you've noticed or want to tell me?' – perhaps even to ask that several times. Meanwhile the doctor needs to keep their eyes on the eyes of the patient, take only the briefest notes and look at ease.

This doesn't take longer than it does to interrupt or jump in too soon. In fact, the other part of that study showed that when a patient was not encouraged to finish their thoughts and to express their fears fully, they got to the end of the interview, walked over to the door and, while turning the knob, said, 'But I didn't tell you about the pains in my chest.'

The doctor then had to begin again. In some cases the diagnosis and treatment the doctor had recommended were changed because of this last bit of vital information. The whole interview in that case took forty minutes. It could have taken twenty.

The principle seems sound everywhere: to take the time to listen thoroughly is to *increase* the total time available to you. Interrupting takes twice as long.

Doctors can also learn about the release of painful feelings. Crying not only helps human beings think more clearly, it also helps our bodies to heal. If doctors would relax in the face of tears or the expression of fear, just let it happen, the patient would very likely think and feel better.

If you are a doctor, consider thinking of yourself as a kind of Thinking Partner for your patients.

Give them respectful, eye-to-eye, easy attention for as long as it takes for them to say everything. It will be the unusual patient, I predict, who will need fifteen or twenty minutes. Most will need less than ten.

When you meet with your colleagues or staff, run your meetings as a Thinking Environment. Periodically ask your staff Incisive Questions like these, suggested by Jenni Hewat, a head nurse in an oncological practice:

- As our mission is top-notch client care, what do you think would make things flow more easily on a day-to-day basis here?
- In the overall scheme of things here, what do you think is the most important, and how do you think we are doing?
- Is there anything standing in the way of your doing your job well?
- What is one thing you have always wanted to tell me to improve your work life here?
- What am I not noticing in this practice, and if you were in my position what would you do about it?

A Thinking Environment for the Doctor Too

It would be a ludicrous understatement to say that as a doctor you work hard. I have heard that some of you are on call in one way or another a hundred hours a week. Many doctors tell me that this fatigue is endemic, that there is a 'culture of exhaustion', even a kind of professional sanction to stay stretched and overworked, that can make it doubly difficult to combat. One young physician told me that she was sure medical school was mostly a culling ground, to see if the students had the metal to withstand inhuman demand and strain. 'I don't remember one doctor in my training ever telling me I did something well,' Chloe said. 'Their appreciation ratio was more like 1 to 5 or on some days 0 to 5. I made it, but lots of brilliant potential doctors didn't. We certainly don't get treated to a Thinking Environment. So how would it ever occur to us now as doctors to create one?'

Few doctors, few people in the health professions in general even, feel they can insist on the chance to stop, sit down and think. But for a moment consider giving yourself the gift of a Thinking Partnership with a colleague or friend. You could talk about anything and this person would be respectful, interested and would not judge you or interrupt you. You could think about your day ahead; you could think out loud about a patient; you could figure out what *you* really think about a sensitive situation at work; or you could cry the grief you feel from a patient's death.

You could occasionally spend fifteen minutes thinking about the successes you have had recently and taking just a second to feel proud of yourself. You could plan your child's weekend or your next holiday or make a shopping list. You could re-think the design of your country's health care. Or you could just sit and not say a thing. You could be still for fifteen whole minutes and notice that the person listening to you respects you and is happy for you just to be docked for a brief moment before the gales begin again.

You are worth anything it takes to stay rested, happy and deeply tuned into the people you serve.

The training Chloe dreams of for physicians is not out of the question.

It is beginning to happen in Sheffield. Jane Fitzgerald, a particularly far-sighted doctor there, is gradually introducing a Thinking Environment into her teaching of GPs and into her own practice. 'The important change,' she says, 'is for medical training to make the creation of a Thinking Environment and the removing of an appendix equal in the mind of the doctor – both essential to healing.'

Some Evidence

I had been recovered from cancer for about fifteen years when a friend of mine with HIV, a doctor himself, introduced me to a medical researcher whose field was immunology. In those early days of the HIV/AIDS epidemic she was following the lives of the people who had lived the longest with AIDS in the USA. She found that they had some interesting things in common.

They all had someone in their life who listened to them without judgement every day for as long as they needed. They all felt loved and appreciated by at least one other person. They all socialized with people who looked at the epidemic from a positive, hopeful perspective. They all were involved directly in some project that embodied their deepest values and in which they could speak with authenticity and conviction. They all had access to the latest correct information about HIV and about the nature of HIV and gay oppression. And they all were allowed to cry and laugh and be angry or scared.

Another striking feature they had in common was that they all 'refused to do unwanted favours'. In other words, they could say no; they could escape from the victim role. They could stay empowered. They could think for themselves.

She observed that those circumstances actually physically balance the immune system. They caused the T helper cells and killer cells and lymphocytes to reproduce in just the right proportions.

I could see that the components of a Thinking Environment had just been corroborated by physical evidence of their healthful effects on the immune system.

And so I think that it is not absurd to assume that a Thinking Environment is essential, both for the mind to think for itself beautifully and for the body to stay ahead of deadly viruses, bacterial infections and degenerative forces that can eventually destroy it. A Thinking Environment may turn out not to be just a thing of the mind and soul, but also a requirement for the body. It would be just like Nature to be that elegant.

CHAPTER 36

Schools

**People learn best
in a large context
of genuine praise.**

The school in Maryland that I co-founded, Thornton Friends School, is committed to many of the principles of a Thinking Environment. Twenty-seven years later the key ingredient of its vision is still respect – for the student as thinker, the student as full human being, the student as responsible, loving, intellectually adroit, academically grounded young adult, committed to making a positive difference in the world. But Thornton is small and at the moment most schools are big.

So until our society can see the importance of making all schools small, with class sizes under fifteen, I recommend that even big schools take whatever steps they can towards becoming Thinking Environments. Adding even one small component can make a big difference.

To teachers, whatever the size of their school, I would say:

- Ask your students what they think five times more often than you tell them what you think.
- Find the *student* interesting even if you are bored to death with their ideas. Do not interrupt them. Find the sound, good ideas in what they say and mention them. And before you comment or give your ideas, ask for more from them.
- When correcting misinformation, do it with a tone and facial expression that says, 'You are intelligent.' If, for example, the student is

studying for a vocabulary test and you say, 'What is the definition of volatile?' and the student says, 'Of one's own free will,' say with a gentle tone and a nod, 'Changeable.' Don't even say, 'No that is not right. The correct definition is "changeable".' And of course don't say, 'No, you stupid, hopeless kid, the definition of volatile is "changeable".' Just give the correct information as if you were handing them the moon.

- Ten minutes before the end of the class, divide students into Thinking Pairs and give them each five minutes to talk without interruption, and with full attention from their partner, about what they have learned in that class and what was confusing to them. In listening to each other they will learn even more.

- Begin the first class of the morning with a quick round of positive comments of some sort from everyone. Questions like: 'What is going well for you?' or 'What did you do yesterday that you feel good about today?' will raise the Thinking Environment to start the day. Remember to give everyone a turn to speak.

- Don't humiliate one student in front of others. Let disciplinary action take place in private.

- Create some way for each student to be concretely appreciated by one of their peers at least once a month. A simple appreciation circle is one way to do that. Everyone says what they particularly respect about the person on their left, for example.

- Provide a mini-course in how to give intelligent, undivided attention to people. At the beginning of the year, require everyone to take that course. A course I recommend for this is one created by Lee Glickstein. The course is called Speaking Circles. The book he has written about it is *Be Heard Now.*

I visited a high school recently where I saw Speaking Circles in action. Ten teenagers gathered for ninety minutes in a small room. Each took a turn to stand in front of the group and talk for five minutes without interruption about absolutely anything at all they wanted to say. They were encouraged not to prepare a speech, not even to know for sure what they would say before they rose to speak. The co-facilitator told me that the students on the course had not ever spoken in front of groups before, that a few of them 'could hardly order at a restaurant'.

Three people in turn said what they thought had been effective in the delivery. The feedback ended with the adult co-facilitator saying she though the speaker had done well. There was absolutely no negative feedback allowed throughout the ninety-minute class. The students were given a tape of their own performance. They would watch it in private and see for themselves what had not been good about their work.

That simple format is teaching those teenagers things few teenagers ever learn in school. The obvious things they are learning are how to speak compellingly in front of their peers, how to stand proudly in front of a group, how to harness the attention of the group by capturing them in quiet at the beginning, how not to fidget, say 'er' or give up, and how to discover what they did think and want to say rather than just memorizing a speech.

Yet even more impressive as far as I am concerned is that they are learning how to give *real attention* to each other without judgement or embarrassment, how to find what is genuinely good in something and say it, how to treat others the way they would like to be treated, how not to interrupt and how to ensure that everyone gets a turn. They are learning some of the components of a Thinking Environment without realizing it.

They also have, this racially and economically diverse group of students, an education in the real socio-historical realities of groups different from themselves. In listening this well to each other they gradually learn, indelibly it seems, the facts, the heartbreaks, the acts of courage, the history, the dreams of people. This learning sticks.

- Apply a five-to-one ratio of appreciation to criticism when you are evaluating students' work. Mention first everything they are doing that has genuine merit. Then find the key area for improvement: that is, the one area which if it were to improve would improve everything else. Be sure they have understood and listen to them without stopping them. Then end the interview with positive comments about them and their work.

I marvel at how a context of appreciation seems to many teachers and academics to mean 'no criticism'. It is as if they think the human mind goes to mush if it is appreciated, as if the criticisms won't be heard if there is any appreciation around. They say, almost immediately after I recommend it, that giving criticism is essential for excellence in scholarship – as if I had said, 'Don't criticize.' However, I didn't say, 'Don't criticize.' I said, '*Criticize in a positive context.* Do it in a Thinking Environment.'

Students' work can improve rapidly if they finish reviewing your corrections with their mind full of accurate, positive impressions of themselves as thinkers, scholars and people and of their work as having real merit even with its flaws.

Just recently I asked Ginger, a yound PhD candidate, about her progress on her thesis. 'Well,' she said, 'I guess it will be OK eventually, if I ever recover from last week.'

She told me about the interview she had had with the head of her PhD committee. 'I wrote that chapter based on all the things she had told me in the last interview and I thought it was good. But when she handed it back to me, it was lacerated with marginalia about what was wrong with it. And while I sat there holding this sad-looking creation of mine, she talked for fifteen minutes about all that was wrong with the research. I agree that I can greatly improve the value of my research. But I am in shreds now. Not because I need to improve it, but because she made me feel that I might as well quit, that I am a terrible scholar and a worse writer. Afterwards I felt no energy for revising it at all.'

What Ginger was describing was a completely unnecessary, gratuitous and harmful principle at work in academia: that if you saturate the student's mind with criticism, they will improve. That evening she saw this professor, who inquired how she was. Ginger said, laughing, 'Still reeling from this afternoon.' The professor said, 'You mean I made you think, huh?'

In fact the professor had done just the opposite. She had made Ginger *not* think. And she could have prevented that so easily. She could have begun with details of what was good in Ginger's chapter. Then she could have told her to broaden the research and make key changes in her writing. Next she could have listened to Ginger and ended the interview with another acknowledgement of her strengths. That would have taken no more time. While communicating what Ginger needed to change, the approach would have left her with energy and eagerness to get back to work on the thesis.

Receiving a cargo of criticism does not build character and discipline. It builds a core of self-doubt and in some people it builds a determination to retaliate, to do the same thing to their graduate students later. To toughen against criticism is not to become more intelligent or creative. To toughen is to tighten. To think well and for yourself requires that your mind be limber. It is I believe the job of teachers to preserve lissomness in the minds of their students while correcting and guiding their work. Both take place together.

Ginger and I did have fun, though, coming up with the limiting bedrock assumption that that interview had embedded in her and designing this Incisive Question to remove it: 'If you knew that you are a fine scholar and writer and an intelligent human being even when your professor is attacking you, how would you feel as you start the next chapter of your dissertation?'

Self-respect and respect for others are two key ingredients of responsible human living that are missing in street gangs, drug groups, 'men who behave badly' and the desperate unemployed youth of our cities. Schools, run as Thinking Environments, could become one antidote to this sagging segment of our nearly-adult society. A Thinking Environment could be established in every school without losing a shred of academic teaching. The Thinking Environment approach is not 'instead of' but a 'means of' teaching both the ever-hallowed basics and advanced-level knowledge and skill.

If we turned our schools into Thinking Environments, imagine what sort of society students from these schools would insist on, what kind of human interactions both at work and at home they would create without fanfare. And imagine what calibre of leaders they might become.

CHAPTER 37

Politics

Democracy can become
a Thinking Environment.

'It applies absolutely,' said Frances Fitzgerald, opposition Minister for Defence in Ireland.

I was sounding discouraged about whether a Thinking Environment could ever be seen to apply to the most committed adversarial arena in our society. Frances was very clear. 'The way we do politics at the moment is not the way we have to do it forever. Democracy is still in the making and we can, we must in fact, evolve it towards a Thinking Environment.

'It is true,' she continued, 'that the traditional culture of politics does not begin to get the best thinking from elected members. Obviously there are the individuals who buck the system. But we are every minute up against the culture that is grounded in aggressive behaviour. It is oppositional at its core. You have to think not about what is right and good, not about new ideas, but about the game: about how to destroy the opposition.

'Parliamentary politics is said to be rooted in debate. But the quality of debate is very low. For example, we don't ask how we can have a truly effective health service. We instead try to destroy the health minister.

'The culture of politics is "Don't say what is on your mind." Saying what you really think is usually dangerous. If you do it, you wait first for the attack from your colleagues and then for the attack from the media. These are not good conditions for thinking well.

'The value each of us brings to politics – the freshness and accuracy of our own perception – is being lost. Politicians begin to wonder whether they are having any effect.

'Also, the assumption that a major political party must speak with one voice is insane. The media inflame this assumption by interpreting dissension as weakness. But we could easily handle the media by saying, "We are moving toward a decision; we are having a most interesting and varied debate. We will hear what everyone thinks and come to the best decision."

'In politics we need to encourage listening. We need to encourage diversity. We need to go for what is true. If there were no difference between what is political and what is true, society would change.

'Yes, all of this is the current state of politics. And we all are impoverished because of it. But elected democratic politics is the best governing system humans have devised so far, and I believe there are ways to bring the principles of democracy together with the principles of a Thinking Environment.

'A Thinking Environment will give us better politics. When I have tried it, it has improved things. Even asking the odd Incisive Question in committees has helped people think better. And the times when we have gone around the committee and given everyone a turn to speak without interruption, we have achieved much better ideas. To see the truth in each other's ideas instead of attacking them wholesale is what makes negotiations successful in the end.

'I remember when John Hume was being vilified for talking with Sinn Fein. "They are terrorists," some politicians angrily said, "You are talking with *terrorists*."

"I hate terrorists as much as you do," John answered, "but to get peace you have to talk with the people you hate."

'I remember one day when the debate was hot about whether or not to support his talks. The view was mounting that we would be attacked if we did. I decided then to ask a question instead of continuing the harangue.

"We may in fact be attacked," I said. "But what if John Hume is right?"

'There was silence. The question had done loads more than a speech would have done.

'I believe that we can bring these two systems together. We just have to use our imagination. If we can invent democracy in the first place, we can figure out how to advance it so that it encourages people's best thinking. That was the original point of democracy anyway, wasn't it?'

Frances is not alone in her view. In England Tessa Jowell, Minister for Public Health, believes the blending of politics and a Thinking Environment is possible too; not easy or immediate, but possible. She introduces the values of a Thinking Environment in lots of ways in Parliament. One was during a committee meeting at Westminster. I like this story because it illustrates how women's culture challenges the rigid rules of behaviour of male-conditioned institutions. One of those rigid rules is that nothing is more important than the organization.

The committee was setting a date for its next meeting. With the first suggestion the minister said, 'I cannot come on that date.' No one spoke. She explained, 'It is my daughter's birthday.' Still no one spoke, so she continued, 'If I miss this next committee meeting, none of you a week later will remember that. But if I miss my daughter's birthday, she will remember that for the rest of her life.' Silence. She said, 'I set my priorities according to those to whom I am irreplaceable.' When the meeting adjourned, another woman MP stopped her in the corridor and thanked her for her honesty. A few minutes after that, another woman did the same. And in the car park one of the older male MPs whispered as he passed her, 'I wish I had had your courage when my daughter was young.'

Another MP in England is exploring ways to change the culture of Parliament so that it is good for human beings. He said to me, 'The day John Smith died Parliament was real in a way I have never seen it. Usually when a member dies, their name is mentioned and we get on with the work. That day we adjourned for a few hours while people dealt with the shock, while they embraced each other, cried, shook their heads, stared into space and drafted statements about John. We then reconvened in the House to pay tribute to him. There was no posturing or plotting. We were simply real with each other. Does it have to take death to give us permission to collaborate and be ourselves?'

In Texas a Thinking Environment was for several years thrust into the middle of the state legislature on a regular basis by Ann Richards, former State Governor. She talked about this in one of her speeches: 'When men in the legislature are asked why they find it difficult sometimes to have a female governor, they say that it is not just because I am assertive and straightforward (in fact, rude on occasion, which I am) and not because I don't give a damn whether they like me or not, which I don't. They say that they find me difficult because I often interrupt the pro- ceedings to say, "Now tell me again, why are we doing it this way?"'

Change of this kind, asking the question, listening, putting people first, giving everyone a turn, threatens the way things have always been.

Another person whose innate understanding of a Thinking Environ- ment is evident is Inez McCormack of Northern Ireland. I was moved by one thing in particular that she said: 'If you base your analysis of organizations on the premise that what matters is the relationship between yourself and one other person, you assert a challenge to the very nature of organizations and this changes the world.'

Do we dare?

CHAPTER 38

Love Relationships

Love deepens
in a Thinking Environment.

Sex is what usually comes to mind when we think of love relationships – and I will get to that, I promise. First, however, I want to suggest that any act of love deepens when it is embraced by the act of thinking for yourself. I do not mean by this that in love you must cultivate cerebral detachment. I mean to suggest that you let your own heart and mind mingle with integrity and then welcome into yourself the heart and mind of someone else.

Some people have described a Thinking Environment as, in itself, an experience of love. I think I know why. To love you have to give attention to another person. At the same time you have to hold on to yourself, never losing yourself in them.

To do both of these things simultaneously you have to be present. You cannot 'wander around', preoccupied with events from yesterday, failings from last month or anxiety about life ahead. When you drift, sucked away by fearful conjecturings, you lose the connection with the other person. If your heart is full of passion but your thoughts are scattered, love is thin. Love grows when your mind is perched right on the edge of this very second.

To be in this present second of life you have to be *you*. You cannot strive to be acceptable. You cannot try to think what the other person thinks, or feel what they feel. Love is the two of you being yourselves, revealing yourselves to each other, nimbly, never losing the integrity of your own thinking or your profound interest in each other.

Love is not at its best when you are slipping on the rocks and being swept out into the other person's identity, ideas and values. Love begins with the act of respect for who you are and is driven by an insatiable desire to know the core of the other person. This means that to be intimate with one another you have to create for each other the conditions in which you both can *keep thinking* – clearly, and for *yourselves*. Love at its best seems not to build fantasies or turn its head. It is intelligent. It does not succumb to wishful thinking. It sees what is there, calls it by name and handles it. Love craves reality. In this state of giving each other attention *and* staying autonomous, love gestates when you say what you really think, bone-deep. It emerges from moments when you do not hold back or dissemble.

I believe that the human heart partnered with the human mind is the juiciest thing imaginable. When someone wants to know what you really think, love can begin. When someone wants to know all of what you think, all of what you feel, when they are respectful of it, fascinated by it, not needing to control it, love grows. On the other hand, the minute someone tries to shape your thoughts for you, love recedes. When someone looks at you, wants you, in order to bend you to fill their fantasy or make them proud or to adorn their ambitions with you, love is doomed.

Love thrives in your words but also in the quiet between you where words cannot camouflage the truth of who you are.

Bringing Love to Life

How can you make these abstract descriptions of love come to life in your days and nights together? You can do very simple things.

You can begin by stopping interruption. If from this moment you never again interrupted each other, you would already have begun a deeper level of attention, connection and respect between you. So begin there. Just stop interrupting each other. Stop particularly the arrogant act of finishing each other's sentences. Instead, enjoy each other's search for your own just-right word or phrase.

Then agree that each evening you will ask about each other's day and listen all the way through without giving advice or making comments. You will pay attention, eyes on the one speaking, until they have said everything. You might find a natural way to ask if there is more too. Be sure that this is reciprocal.

Then start letting each other cry, or talk about anger or fear without patching it up for each other. Touch or hold each other possibly, but not too tight, not in order to smother away the pain but just enough to let it stream off in its own way. Don't be frightened if the tears go on a while. They will eventually stop and the sun will pour in.

My husband Christopher and I agreed when we got married that we would spend our evenings and our weekends together as a sacred time, rarely to be co-opted by work. Before we married he lived in England and I lived in the USA. We saw each other in intense fortnights every two or three months, and so to ease the pain of separation and to build our relationship day to day we talked on the phone almost every day for seven years.

I was reminded once about how true Christopher and I were to giving each other an equal turn to talk when, after our phone call at my colleague Sara's house one evening, she said to me, 'Well! I thought maybe you had died or something. First I felt sorry for Christopher because you were talking so much you hardly drew breath. That lasted a good fifteen minutes I think. Then suddenly I couldn't hear anything. That went on for ages too. So I peeked into the room to see if you were still breathing and saw you sitting there nodding and smiling. You weren't saying much. I think you grunted or said yes and exclaimed enthusiastically a couple of times. But I had never seen anything like it. Then I realized – you must be taking turns talking and listening. You really, actually, do do that don't you?'

Now that we have the luxury of living together, those ways of being with each other – usually attentive, not interrupting, asking questions that keep each other thinking and talking – are just the way life is for us. And almost every evening, regardless of how exhausting or tense our work day has been, we close out the world, make a fire and a simple supper and talk and listen to each other approximately in equal turns until we have said everything we want to about anything. Sleep, after that kind of sharing, is sweet.

We have no young children and that makes all of this easier, of course. But many couples I know who do have children find ingenious ways to block out special time together most evenings. It can be done. It just has to be important enough to factor into what one friend calls their family needs matrix!

Another couple I know plans one day and overnight away together each month. Another keeps Saturday mornings as theirs, off limits to children or pressure.

Do try it. Just sit down together, be still, give each other relaxed, full attention and approximately equal turns, and listen. You will find that very little can replace it or equal it.

A shocking study of couples who live together tracked their focused listening time to an average of eight seconds. See if you can improve on that average. Then push it. Listen without interruption or distraction for five minutes, then ten. Love is this simple to nurture.

And, starting today if you can, tell each other precisely what you admire, respect, even adore in each other. Do this every day without fail – and always after an argument; during it if humanly possible. Restrict your criticisms to one fifth of all your interactions.

When things get difficult between you, take many short turns each back and forth to talk and listen. Propose changes more often than you complain.

I work with couples some of the time, and I never fail to be impressed with how much good comes from a very little change in the way they relate to each other. I recommend that they do the things I have mentioned above and with even a few of them in place they know deeper love than ever before. And that is all before we ever talk about sex.

There is a group of couples in Burleson, Texas, with whom I have worked for several years. They meet monthly at one of their houses. They have a meal and then a two-hour support group of 'doing Thinking Environment things'. Their format is simple and works impressively:

1 They each take a turn around the group to say something positive that has happened in their life and their marriage during the past month.

2 Then they go off in couples to private corners and take ten-minute turns each saying anything at all about any topic of their choice: their day, their job, their worries, their dreams, their children. The listener never interrupts, comments or asks questions. They listen, keeping their eyes on their partner's eyes.

3 Then they re-convene as a group and one person takes a turn to discuss something of their choice in depth. Someone assumes the role of the Thinking Partner and listens through Part 1 and then, if asked, helps the person to identify and remove assumptions that are still blocking them.

4 Then they go back into couples and do a Timed Talk about a topic of concern to them both. They take three-minute turns back and forth for thirty minutes.

5 They then take five minutes each to appreciate each other with no whisper of criticism. Topics which are good catalysts for appreciation include: why I am glad I married you; why I am proud of you when we are in public; what you do as a lover that I love; ways I think you are a good parent; what I miss most about you when you are away.

6 The evening ends with everyone saying what was good in the evening and appreciating out loud the person on their right.

One of the couples says that this monthly format has saved their marriage, without question. Another says it helps counteract the way the world just never lets you do this sort of thing, the way life closes in and busy takes the place of close. Another, who were given the Thinking Environment course as a wedding present, has never known marriage without it and can't imagine life, as they put it, 'without this richness and depth'.

Love and Sex

Sex is not often talked about as an act of thinking. Too often sex is thought of as a mindless act of abandon with no room for thinking at all. However, sometimes sex and love entwine in a Thinking Environment, and when they do, that *is* heaven.

If you want love and sex to deepen in bed, spend lots of time establishing a Thinking Environment between the two of you out of bed first. Then take the ten components to bed with you.

- While you make love, pay attention to each other every minute. Listen to each other. Talk to each other.
- Ask each other questions occasionally, such as 'What would be good for you right now?'
- Notice your equality. Take turns giving each other focused attention.
- Say what is good five times more than you criticize. Say what you enjoy about each other. Say 'I love you'. Touch each other so awarely that you cannot 'wander away'.
- Don't compete, with each other or with each other's past. Enjoy each other in the present.
- Allow each other to express feelings, even to cry.
- Set up the place with special care to say back to you both, 'You matter.'
- Before you ever make love, give each other accurate information: about your history, your HIV status, about contraception, about scars on your body or bits that embarrass you, about what is sexy to you, about what would make things best between you.

- Set aside negative assumptions about each other's identity. Enjoy your differences.
- In the centre of your passion let there be ease.

Passion built from the magic of giving each other attention of this quality, the kind of attention that frees the mind to be itself and the heart to open fully, is extraordinary. Sex is particularly sexy when it is an experience every minute of thinking for yourself.

Love and thinking need each other.

CHAPTER 39

Families

Families are
the first
Thinking Environment.

My favourite greetings card says, just under a water-colour sketch of reeds, 'The best thing you can do for your children is to listen to them.'

During a question period after a talk I gave for a large corporation, one of the managers asked me, 'How can I make sure my new baby can think for herself when she is grown up? How can I protect her from other people's behaviour that damages confidence in one's own mind?'

'You can't,' I said. 'But you can do this: give her attention as if she were a work of art. She is. Tell her countless times a day that you love her and respect her. Let her cry. And as soon as possible, ask her what she really thinks, *every day*. Then listen like mad.'

The importance of listening to your children cannot be stressed enough.

One of my friends is pregnant for the first time. She asked me what I thought was a worthy goal of parenthood. Not surprisingly, I said that I thought a worthy goal would be to create a Thinking Environment in the family. That would mean treating your children and each other as consistently as possible with the Thinking Environment principles. For example, it would mean praising your children five times more than you criticize them. That would change most families right there. If you want your children to become clear-thinking adults with their own mind, appreciate them as children. Of course, you will have to correct them and be firm with them as you teach and guide them, but appreciate them far more.

Do Not Infantilize Your Children

Treating your children to a Thinking Environment means not infantilizing them, even when they are infants. That probably means speaking to them from the day they are born with as much respect and intelligibility as you would to any adult. It probably means not talking baby talk to them, not saying things in words or tones that you would be embarrassed to use to someone of your own age. It is possible to be expressive, even wildly affectionate, to children without talking to them, even as infants, as if they had no brain.

Not infantilizing our children also means asking what dreams reside in their soul. It means paying attention to them without urgency, listening to them with fascination, showing them that they will not be interrupted, that they will not be humiliated even when they go out on a limb with a wacky idea.

Families as Meetings

Not infantilizing our children also means including them in important family discussions before decisions are made. It means giving them each a turn to say what they think and then being quiet while they speak. It means recognizing that families are organizations too and have meetings as surely as any corporate team. Families are where group dynamics begin. Family 'meetings' can shape or shatter individual dreams. Organizations just follow suit.

In fact, the place where meetings occur most frequently and have the biggest impact on people is in families. You might not think of your family dinners as meetings or your fights or bedtime talks or your weekend trips as meetings, but, formally or not, that is what they are. You gather, talk about issues that concern you all and decide what to do.

How those 'meetings' are run can influence how all of you feel about each other. How people are treated in those 'meetings' can determine how well or poorly they think for the rest of the day, and even for the rest of their life. Too many children go off to school, and too many parents go off to work, broken apart by lousy family 'meetings' that dominated breakfast.

Marley's family has formal family meetings. On one occasion the four of them gathered in the living room to talk about television, a tense issue. For two years they had not had a TV. Marley and her husband Robert had taken it out of the house when they saw that the two children were hardly ever reading or playing games or doing fantasy play any more. Moshi, their son, however, had been saving his pocket money and earnings from little jobs and now wanted a Nintendo. He was dangerously close to being able to afford it. He and his sister Anya had been collecting catalogues for months, pouring over the TV and video games sections. They approached their mother.

'Let's have a meeting with all of us to discuss this,' they said to her.

That meant the four of them around the table. Everyone would have a turn and no one would interrupt. They began.

'Should Moshi get a video game set and if so what will that mean about TV in the house?' Marley said to clarify the discussion item.

Moshi said, 'It will mean having a TV because you have to have it for the monitor of the games. And I think we should be able to watch TV now at least a little.'

Anya said, 'I don't want it on all the time, though. I kind of like not having the noise, like a boring other person in the house.'

Robert said, 'I don't see how we can stop it from dominating the house. I know how that happens. You think it won't and then it does. In the Samuels' house the TV is on all of the time.'

Marley said, 'You two have just got back your imagination. Nothing is going to convince me to surrender that to TV again.'

Then discussion ensued. 'OK,' said Moshi, 'then why don't we say that it can be on only at certain hours. Like let's say before dinner after we have done our homework.' No one interrupted. He went on, 'Maybe for an hour?'

'But what if I want to watch a movie or something and you want to play with the games?' asked Anya.

'Well, how about each morning we decide on the way to school what we will do that night? And let's start with getting a half hour each.'

Robert said, 'That's good but who turns it off?'

'We will,' said Anya.

'Yeah, we will and you guys have to trust us,' added Moshi.

'And if you don't turn it off? What kind of punishment should there be?'

'There shouldn't be any,' said Anya. 'Punishments just make you feel bad and angry and like keeping it on more.'

'Well, consequences, then,' said Marley.

'I don't like this discussion right now because you are changing everything. Moshi and I don't like TV as a way of life either, remember? We are not like the Samuels. And just because we want an hour a day doesn't mean we will become stupid couch potatoes just like that or even ever. Don't assume the worst all the time.'

'This once,' said Marley.

'Let's try it,' said Robert.

They agreed to meet a week later to assess the result of the trial. So far the plan is working, though Marley is nervous about how long the discipline can last. 'But I'm pretty certain that if the kids had not had an equal share in the discussion, they would not be as in charge of making the agreement work,' she said.

Even very young children who are not going to 'vote' on most of the family decisions can enjoy equality *as thinkers* in a family. As a parent you can establish ways of being with your children so that they know you respect their minds as much as your own.

I remind Marley occasionally that she is doing a successful job of creating a Thinking Environment for her children. She shakes her head when I say this. Parents are quick to take the blame for their children's behaviour and slow to take the credit.

This process of turning 'meetings', whether they be formal or unrecognizably impromptu, into a Thinking Environment is, if anything, more important in families than in organizations; and, not surprisingly, it is harder. More is at stake in families and more is gained. Hearts are closer to the ground there, more easily flattened and more easily found.

What Sex Is It?

From the time anyone knows there is a baby on the way, it is being categorized. People want to know whether it is a boy or a girl. They want to feel comfortable making assumptions about how it will behave and look and feel. Before the child has a chance it is already being defined by the world's assumptions about what girls and boys should and should not be. And as you could see from Chapter 12, those gender assumptions have a dangerous impact on the way people treat each other and thus on the quality of a Thinking Environment.

Not infantilizing our children would, therefore, mean encouraging boys and girls to develop each other's cultures. It would mean encouraging them equally to feel and be brave, to collaborate and to shine, to be generous and to take up space, to be gentle with their bodies and to strengthen them, to listen and to speak, to praise and to correct and, most important of all, to think for themselves.

It would mean showing them how the messages of boys' conditioning destroy a Thinking Environment. It would mean helping them figure out how to stop male conditioning in their peer group without losing all their friends. It would mean teaching our girls not to follow male conditioning as a leadership model but also not to confuse male conditioning with males themselves, and to assert the values of women's culture in their own leadership.

Asking Incisive Questions

Not infantilizing our children would mean finding out what they are assuming when they are unable to think clearly and then removing their assumption with an Incisive Question. I watched a young English mother, Anne, do approximately this with her six-year-old daughter.

I was sitting at Anne's kitchen table. Her daughter Jennifer was just about ready to go to school, putting on her little coat and mittens. She looked up at Anne who was leaning over, ready to give her a kiss, and she said, 'Mummy, what do I do about Hamish?'

'What about Hamish?' asked Anne, buckling Jennifer's coat belt.

'He said I am stupid yesterday.' I thought I saw that mother's look on Anne's face that said, 'Why do kids invariably wait until two seconds before they have to be out the door before they raise huge issues affecting their hearts?'

But Anne smiled and said, 'Well, honey, what do you think you should do?'

Jennifer said, 'I don't know. That is why I asked you.'

Anne stood up. She looked at me. I smiled.

Anne turned back to Jennifer. 'Sweetie, if you knew that you are not stupid, that in fact you are very intelligent, no matter what Hamish says, what would you do about him today?'

Jennifer slipped on her other mitten. 'Oh,' she said, surprisingly perky, 'well, I would let him use the red brush, I guess. I wouldn't say he would have to play somewhere else forever.'

'Good,' Anne said in a tone that revealed confusion and no time to get the details.

'OK,' Jennifer said and they made it out the door and down the steps just as the school bus door was opening.

Not bad, I thought. I wonder how long that would have taken if Anne had tried to tell Jennifer what to do and had poured on a mother's reassuring, discountable statements about Jennifer's not being stupid.

A family that is a Thinking Environment is a haven where people are asked routinely what they really think and get to say it. It is also where they are not told what to feel, but are allowed to say when they are afraid and when they are angry, or to skip and leap with uncontainable delight and not be called a fool. It is a place where cuddles are frequent and physical touching always boundaried and respectful.

No Violence

It is also a place free of the threat of physical violence or punishment. Spanking, slapping and beating stop people from thinking. They are as humiliating for a child as they would be for you, an adult. Can you imagine condoning beatings between you and your spouse, or you and your neighbour?

If adult physical abuse is part of your family life, and it is for more families than you might imagine, it is without your endorsement, isn't it? You probably do not say to your children, 'It is good for daddy to hit me. That is the best way to settle disputes with people when you are older. We hope you will learn from us about communicating this way.' But many people who think it is bad to hit their spouse or their neighbour think it is fine to hit their children. And they do so as a matter of family policy. Some people actually still think that children learn to behave better if their bad behaviour meets with violence. But good behaviour is not what they learn from violence. They learn violence from violence. They learn humiliation and self-hatred. And we wonder why we have so many street gangs, so much hit-and-run neighbourhood vandalism and continued drug pushing – and murder.

What people – of any age – learn from violence, including verbal violence, is to dominate in order to win, not to listen, not to think, not to negotiate or come to agreement with people. Physical punishment strips the components of listening, dignity, ease, equality, Incisive Questions and expression of feelings out of the environment and injects into it fear, shame, inferiority, urgency, interruption, denigration and misinformation. Physical punishment also installs limiting bedrock assumptions like 'I am bad, I deserve rejection and pain, life is unsafe, you can't trust anyone, it is best to avoid punishment and not to try to achieve anything, revenge is the way to feel good again.'

To hit or yell at someone is to infantilize them, to make them feel 'like children', like inferiors. It is to make them obey, it is to stop them from thinking for themselves. To listen to someone, to take respectful turns discussing the issue until you reach an unforeseeable, good agreement is to dignify you both, to keep you both thinking clearly and acting responsibly.

So what do you do with toddlers who run for the fifth time out into the street? See to it that they don't. Take them away from the traffic. Explain to them about it and then set up play for them somewhere else. Then when they are old enough to reason, teach them about traffic and safety. Be firm, but do not hit them, or yell at them. We do not want our children to grow up prey to the seductive requirements of obedience from narcissistic adults. But that requires years of being treated with respect for their own good mind, being praised for their loving heart.

Families do not have to have lots of money to become Thinking Environments. They don't have to live anywhere fancy or large, take ski trips or give big parties. They simply have to treat each other as if each of them mattered profoundly.

I know one family that usually manages to have evening meals together (a modern anomaly). At the beginning of the meal somebody always asks everyone to say what went well in their day and then what didn't go so well. Each person, including the parents, has a turn while the others listen. After that, ordinary conversation begins. At that point it looks pretty much like any family dinner except that there is somehow more respect around the table, a connection most family meals lack.

Worry

Worry and family life seem bound by definition. We feel in fact almost obligated to worry about our children, and our children, surprisingly, worry about us. However, worry anywhere is a set-back to thinking. It does not help. It just mires us.

Worry is almost always the product of an assumption, a parasite in our mind. If you ask yourself, 'What am I assuming right now that is causing me to worry?' you will know immediately and you can remove the assumption by asking an Incisive Question. Almost always the worry will recede.

Lucy said to me, 'I am a wreck between nine and midnight every weekend. Spencer is now seventeen and we have an agreement that he will come home from his evenings out between nine and midnight. He is good about it. He has not yet actually been more than five minutes late. So I should just trust him. But I don't. I worry instead.

'And that means that every Friday and Saturday night I am in knots and sweats for almost the whole evening. I don't have any fun. I just think about him and watch the clock. It is exhausting. When he does come home, I am relieved but also resentful. A part of me is angry at him for putting me through that even though he didn't. I did.'

'What are you assuming,' I asked her, 'that makes you worry so intensely between nine and midnight?'

'That he is dead in an alley somewhere.'

You wouldn't have had to be a genius to predict that answer. Even as she said it, I was wondering how on earth I would deal with it. Staying true to the session model I would have to recognize it as a possible-fact assumption and try to find the bedrock assumption beneath it. But I did not know if I could bring myself to say, 'That's possible. But what might you be assuming that is making that worry you so intensely?' Wouldn't it seem like the most callous, dumbo question in the world? Nonetheless I decided to try, because not once has asking that question failed to reveal a deadly assumption which can be removed and produce freedom on the spot.

'That's possible,' I said, 'Spencer might be lying dead in an alley. But what might you be assuming that makes that worry you so intensely?'

Lucy looked at me with that look that says, 'OK, I will trust you, but only just.' Then she became very still. I waited.

It could have been a full minute later when she said, 'I am assuming that I have no purpose in life without my son, that if he dies I might as well not exist.' She put her head in her hands and sighed. 'No wonder . . .'

When she looked up, I said, 'What is your positive opposite of "have no purpose and might as well not exist?"'

She said, 'I guess it is that my life has its own core.' (Isn't it satisfying to get their words?)

'If you knew,' I asked slowly and softly, 'that your life has its own core, how would you feel between nine and midnight each weekend?'

'I would relax,' she answered. 'I would read or watch a comedy or go out, for God's sake. Mainly, I would not think about the clock until 11.59. I would know in my gut, not just my head, that to worry about Spencer is not going for a second to prevent his dying in an alley. Not for a second. So I would let go. Somewhere inside me I would let go, somewhere where I have not set foot for many years.'

Part Four

A Thinking Future

CHAPTER 40

For the Sake of Our Dreams

Until we are free
to think for ourselves,
our dreams are not free
to unfold.

There are times now and then when the sheer beauty of the human mind at work sweeps me away. Those times usually have to do with possibility, with making our dreams come true.

I have listened to people start what they thought was pure indulgence in idealism and find, because they were in a Thinking Environment, that their mind forged a path to something real. Dreams for a better world reside in most of us, I would guess, dreams that are choked first by people's ridicule and then by the demands of daily life. But our dreams don't die. They sleep, waiting for the right conditions to come along and entice them awake.

Eric's Thinking Session was such a time. I tell you this story changing a few terms. But the story is true.

After Kyle's session (Chapter 25) and after the coffee break, Kyle took on the role of Thinking Partner. 'What do you want to think about, Eric?' he asked.

'There is something I can't stop thinking about,' Eric said slowly. 'No matter what I do I can't get it out of my head. Maybe if I talk about it I will be able to forget it.'

Kyle paid attention to Eric beautifully and did not speak.

'A few months ago I went to northern Uganda. Other microbiologists and I were sent to test a drug – on 6,000 children there. The disease was betahaemolytic streptococcus – less technically: a quick killer of children. Tens of thousands die every five to ten years of this thing. There is a 60 per cent fatality rate and a 75 per cent rate of severe damage to the central nervous system. Any lucky survivors are left deaf and blind. We went to Africa because there was not enough of this disease in concentrated populations in the West to test it on. 'I can't stop thinking about what happened there.'

Kyle kept his attention on Eric.

'When we arrived there,' Eric went on, 'finally in the epicentre, I saw literally hundreds of children comatose. Their spinal fluid, when we tested it, was thick and white, not light yellow and watery the way healthy spinal fluid is. And there was hardly life in those little bodies. Hundreds and hundreds of nearly-dead children were everywhere throughout one village and on into the next one and the next.

'We set up hygienic places to inject this new drug-candidate and began. And this is what gets me.' He tossed his head back to keep tears away and then looked at Kyle. Kyle smiled and nodded to Eric to go on. He kept his eyes on Eric's eyes.

'Within twenty-four hours those children were up, running, laughing, playing with each other, almost as if nothing had been wrong the day before. If I hadn't developed and administered that drug myself, I would have called it a miracle. And as a person of faith, I would have liked to.

'Those children and nearly 3,000 more after them and more after them just got up and lived; they laughed and raced around. They played games and took naps and woke up. My mind can't let that go. The children would have been dead if we had not gone.'

He looked around the room. Everyone was still. He looked at Kyle. Kyle did not speak. He just paid attention to Eric, and Eric spoke again.

'The fact that the cyprocillin worked and so quickly, though, is not what I can't stop thinking about. What haunts me is that we left.'

Eric was quiet for a few seconds, just looking at Kyle, thinking. Busy, but quiet.

'We just left. We had made our determination, so we came back home. We did leave behind the rest of that drug sample but I knew as we got on to the plane that the sample would be gone in a few weeks and that 10,000 more children would die within a month.

'And even *that* is not what is so hard to forget. It's what happened during the flight home. I kept seeing those children nearly dead and then, nearly overnight, playing in the street. My lab buddies and I talked about it almost non-stop for a few hours. We even sort of strategized about the possibility of producing enough cyprocillin to prevent tens of thousands of deaths of children every year. We agreed that cyprocillin could conceivably wipe out the betahaemolytic strain and eliminate the disease from Uganda, maybe even from the face of the earth.

'And then Charles, my direct boss, leaned over and said, "You are naive, Eric. This company is not going to produce massive amounts of cyprocillin to give away at this stage. It just isn't. Industry isn't like that. And pretty soon you would know it because you wouldn't have a job. We did what we did, and that was good. We found out the drug works. That is what we were sent there to do. But for now that is the end of it."

'I felt furious hearing that. It couldn't really be true that money could prevent the chance to wipe out the beta strain there completely. But Charles shook his head and went back to reading his magazine.'

Eric's face was red and his hands were shaking. Kyle smiled at him when he looked up. Kyle did not interrupt even though he had a hundred questions and lots of feelings himself.

'We did our tests,' Eric said slowly as if trying to piece together bits of mosaic. 'They worked. And now we can package and sell the drug to countries that can pay for it, countries where the disease is nothing like as bad, nothing like. This is success.

'What I know in my heart is that this is failure. I think this because we now know that betahaemolytic streptococcus is a completely preventable disease. We could, I am virtually certain, wipe out this disease and all its related permutations, including forms of TB and malaria, throughout Africa and lots of other places if money were not an issue.

'When I got back to the company, I would bring it up, but even they started saying things like, "Forget it, Eric. There's nothing we can do."'

Eric looked back at Kyle. Eric did not speak. This time he was not 'busy'. He had clearly come to a stop.

'That's all. That's all I can think of to say,' he said.

So Kyle said, 'Is there any more you want to say about this?'

'Well, only that I feel completely alone. Am I a fool to keep thinking about this? Probably there is nothing I can do. The guys are probably right. Why can't I just accept that?'

Kyle did not answer. But he paid attention.

'I am young,' Eric said, almost in a whisper. He looked at Kyle again. 'But my life will never be the same. That is the problem. I can't undo the fact that I saw what I saw and know what I know. It makes me sad. And angry.' He looked at Kyle. His eyes dulled again. 'That's all.'

'Let me ask you again just in case you think of more. What else do you think or feel about any of this – does anything more come to mind?'

A flash went across Eric's face and Kyle was glad he had asked.

'Yeah, I don't want to die not having at least tried every possible way to get this drug where it is needed most. I don't want to tell my unborn children that I saved my job but didn't save those lives. I *do* want to do something. I don't want to think of a way to forget it.'

He sat forward on the chair and put his hand in his back jeans pocket. He pulled out a handkerchief and wadded it up into his palm. 'I just can't think what to do.'

He looked up, his eyes red. 'That's all.' Again the stare.

'Well, just in case,' Kyle said, 'is there anything more that comes to mind about this, that you want to say?'

'No, nothing else. That's it.'

'Are you sure?' Kyle asked casually.

'I am sure,' he said, his tone flaccid.

'OK. So now, at this point, what would you like this session to achieve?' Kyle asked him.

Eric shifted in his seat and leaned back, stretching out his legs and breathing out.

'Well, if it could, I guess I would like the session to show me a way to do something about this. Yeah, I would like to find out if I am totally alone in this, to think of how to find like-minded people to discuss it with.'

Kyle was thinking of at least five different ways Eric could find like-minded people to discuss this with. He was aching to suggest what Eric could do. He also wanted to say, 'Of course you must do something about this, Eric, don't let it go; and of course there are like-minded people out there . . .' But he didn't. He waited. He kept paying attention.

Eric went on. 'My manager hasn't said anything to me at all about it since we came back. I don't think his direct boss cares about this. And I certainly wouldn't expect anyone higher up than that to think that freebies to the Third World is such a hot idea. My wife is kind of interested, but she is a sociologist, if you know what I mean.'

His eyes lifeless again, Eric looked at Kyle.

So Kyle asked, 'What might you be assuming that could be stopping you from finding like-minded people to discuss this with?'

Eric was quiet for a few seconds. He looked out into the general space of the seminar room.

'I guess I am assuming that I alone cannot do anything.' He paused and looked across the room at the one live plant. 'Yeah, I am assuming I alone cannot do anything.'

Kyle did not then say, as he was very tempted to do, that all he would have to do was put the word out and people would respond. He did not say, 'Of course you alone can do something, Eric. All big things begin with one person deciding they can do *something*.' He knew Eric wouldn't believe him if he did.

Instead he noted that Eric's assumption was not possible. Out of 30,000 people in the company and out of thousands more people in the field of epidemiology there simply of course were some whom he alone could find to talk with about this blatantly important issue. The assumption 'I alone cannot do anything' was not true. It was a limiting bedrock assumption about how life works.

Kyle knew that Eric's bedrock assumption was absurd, but he did not belittle it. For Eric it was an immobilizing barrier. Never mind that he was a brilliant microbiologist with deafening numbers of PhDs working for one of the top industries in the world. He was tortured. And the assumption that he alone could do nothing was keeping him tortured.

So Kyle asked, 'Eric, if you knew that you alone *can* do something, how would you go about finding like-minded people to discuss this with?'

Eric frowned. 'You'll have to ask me that one more time,' he said. 'I didn't quite follow you.'

'If you knew that you alone *can* do something, how would you go about finding like-minded people to discuss this with?'

Eric looked away and as before was quiet. Busy.

Kyle did not say anything.

Eventually Eric 'came back'. Slowly he said, as if examining an artefact, 'If I really knew that I alone *can* do something . . .' He looked up. 'I would talk to my manager's direct boss instead of assuming he is not interested. And I would talk with his boss because I don't actually know

245

what she thinks. And with the clinical managers. I mean, I don't actually know what any of these people think about this.' He stopped. He looked back at Kyle.

'Let me ask you again,' Kyle said. 'If you knew that you alone *can* do something, how would you go about finding like-minded people to discuss this with?'

Eric laughed. 'I would call the vice-president's office and make an appointment.' He shook his head. 'Nah, I don't know about that one. But actually, how bad could it be? The worst thing that could happen is that he would refuse to see me. Or, if he did meet with me, he might tell me to stop being a fool and get back to the lab.' Eric laughed again and looked around the room. 'That wouldn't be the end of the world. I don't think he would fire me. Not for just having a wild, naive idea.'

Kyle waited until Eric looked at him, clearly stalled, and then said, 'I'll ask you again. If you knew that you alone *can* do something, how else might you go about finding like-minded people to discuss this with?'

'Well, I'd just put out a company e-mail about it and see who responded. If even 1 per cent said yes, I'd have 30 meetings!'

They both laughed. He stopped, so Kyle said, 'And again, if you knew that you alone *can* do something, how else would you find like-minded people to discuss this with?'

'Well, hey, I could put the idea on the Web and see what happened. Maybe lots of people are thinking about stuff like this. I am sure, now that I think about it, that I could not possibly be the first person in the history of industry and epidemics to have a concern like this.'

His eyes were sparkling now. The capillaries in his face made a kind of glow in his cheeks. Blood flows better when the mind is free.

'And again, if you knew that you alone . . .'

'I could find someone who could calculate what it would cost to produce enough cyprocillin to wipe out this disease in Uganda. I could then talk with someone about what sort of financial benefit could result from the publicity if the world found out that this company had generously used its resources to wipe out beta strep. Also how whether or not that kind of caring reputation coupled with the company's excellent science reputation might raise the stock prices or something.'

Eric looked at Kyle. Kyle smiled and just kept paying attention. Eric was thinking for himself with no turning back now. Kyle found it a pleasure to watch. He said later that ordinary conversations, even brainstorming, were not like this.

'Also, there is probably some way to spend less producing massive amounts of the drug going to a concentrated place than we do on vats of it packaged for distribution in paying countries. And we will make the same money on it from the paying countries as we would have anyway.

'I don't know that much about the economics of the thing, but somebody will. Somebody *likes* to figure stuff like that out.'

He smiled at Kyle. 'This is kind of fun,' he said.

Kyle smiled and nodded. 'You're doing a great job,' he said. 'And how else might you find like-minded people to discuss this with if you knew that you alone *can* do something?'

'Well,' Eric said, looking away, 'well, if I really knew that, I might talk with someone in the State Department or maybe the WHO to see if the whole project could be funded outside the company.'

He leaned forward again and lifted his eyes, impaling Kyle's. 'I can be the *catalyst*. I don't have to know everything or convince each person. I just have to keep asking and meeting with people and trying everything I can think of. I just have to keep going until we find a way. Man, Kyle, if we are smart enough to discover the compound and develop this candidate in the first place, we are definitely smart enough to find a way to save those children and not go broke.'

Kyle wanted to dance. He wanted to hug Eric. But he just smiled and nodded and looked pleased. Then he said, 'Shall I ask you one more time?'

Eric shook his head and laughed. 'No, please don't. I've got enough ideas to keep me awake all night.'

'OK,' Kyle said, 'then write down the question so you won't forget it.'

He got out paper and pencil and started writing, saying it out loud as he wrote. 'If there were people out there who . . .'

Kyle said, 'If I knew that I alone *can* do this . . .'

'Oh, yeah,' said Eric, 'how would I convince these people . . .'

'How would I go about finding like-minded people to discuss this with?' Kyle corrected.

'Yeah, that's it,' Eric said. 'God, how could I forget that simple question? You asked me enough times. Why is it again that we forget the stupid question so fast?'

Kyle looked around the circle at me. 'Because the question is not stupid,' I said. 'It is anti-stupid. It is as precise a construction for your dilemma as cyprocillin is for betahaemolytic streptococcus. It was constructed exactly to do away with the assumption that was stopping you from thinking and to produce a brand-new avenue for your mind.'

Everyone was quiet.

Eric closed his notebook. 'Magic,' he said softly.

'No, not magic,' I said, 'science.'

Eric is working on this slowly but steadily, hopeful that he will help find a way to get that drug back to Uganda and some kind of profit back into his company. He is just that determined.

So are lots of us. But without the time and structure to think for ourselves we lose track of what we really want to do for our world. We find no way to put our dreams into action. Or we churn and grow cynical. A Thinking Environment is one dependable way to resurrect our dreams and move them step by step towards reality. As children we understood this. The frightened caution of adulthood had not yet consumed us. Our fantasies were bold.

Do you remember, in fact, when you were little and sometimes played alone? Do you remember, when no one was watching you, the way you talked with your imaginary playmates and how sure you were that the gang of you could do anything? Do you remember not being cautious at all for just an afternoon or two?

I do. I used to do it while 'serving tea' on a blanket under the willow tree in our front garden. My dolls and I used to look straight up to the sky, that big west Texas sky my mother loved so much, right through the willow leaves, and talk and talk about what we were going to do some day.

Mary, my favourite doll because she had real hair, was going to be a geologist and get right inside rocks to understand them. And Jessica was going to live at the very, very tip top of the poplar tree and tell everyone below to stop fighting and start making soup. And I, well, I was going to do something quite wonderful with someone across the ocean who kept sending me love letters.

As children, given a few moments alone and without direction, we know something. As adults we can decide to know it again. We *can* think for ourselves. And, best of all, we can help each other to do that.

For the sake of our dreams, we must.

A Tribute to Diana, Princess of Wales

It is unusual, if not oxymoronic, for global icons to help people think for themselves. When it does occur, something simple and profound happens inside us. And something real and grounding, something surprisingly un-iconish, happens in them as well. It is important to notice this when it takes place and to appreciate it. A year now after her death, I want to pay Diana, Princess of Wales, that tribute.

I believe that her 'particular magic' was that she was able, without having ever been trained, to create in an instant a Thinking Environment for people.

On many occasions I watched her give unfailingly the highest-calibre attention to people. I watched her look into their eyes, bend one knee slightly, rest her arms easily in front of her, relax and listen as if they were the only person in the world at that moment. Often she had literally only a moment, but in a split second, because of the quality of her attention, she disarmed feelings of nervousness and assumptions of inferiority and allowed people to remember that they matter.

I recall the way she entered a room filled with people. Her only thought seemed to be to make a real connection with each of them as soon as possible. She immediately moved close, not waiting for people to be brought to her. She was interested in them. She wanted to know what they thought and how they felt. She could transform a crowd of nerves into laughter and ease just with the way she asked and listened. Her focus was on them, not on herself.

She virtually leapt from the car that way too. Almost, it seemed, before the wheels had stopped, she was reaching with her hand and her eyes and her interest to the person greeting her, creating for them a moment, in the midst of royal protocol, to be themselves.

I watched people become more and more articulate in the light of her real and respectful, unhurried attention. This, I believe, is what people miss. People called it her love, as indeed it was; but in practical terms that love was her natural ability to create for each person an environment in which they could, even if for only a moment, think and speak for themselves. This is perhaps the most dignifying thing one person can do for another. It can be done without designer clothes, without a model's face and figure, without, as she proved, a royal title.

In memoriam I thank the Princess for this. She modelled this calibre of attention, individual to individual, as the world watched. For the world that quality of attention was startling. For her it was just the way life was. I would like to think that one day it can become that for us all.

Index